Karl Marx

Lew Kerbel's Monument to Karl Marx at the Stadthalle (City Hall) in Chemnitz.
Source: Tomasz Mysluk © Dorling Kindersley/Dorling Kindersley Media Library.

William A. Pelz

Elgin Community College

Karl Marx

A World to Win

THE LIBRARY OF WORLD BIOGRAPHY

Series Editor: Peter N. Stearns

Prentice Hall

Boston Columbus Indianapolis New York San Francisco Upper Saddle River
Amsterdam Cape Town Dubai London Madrid Milan Munich Paris Montreal Toronto
Delhi Mexico City Sao Paulo Sydney Hong Kong Seoul Singapore Taipei Tokyo

Editorial Director: Craig Campanella
Executive Editor: Jeff Lasser
Editorial Project Manager: Rob DeGeorge
Editorial Assistant: Julia Feltus
Senior Marketing Manager: Maureen E. Prado Roberts
Marketing Assistant: Samantha Bennett
Operations Specialist: Renata Butera
Cover Designer: Karen Salzbach
Creative Art Director: Jayne Conte
Cover Photo: Library of Congress
Full-Service Project Management: Shiny Rajesh
Composition: Integra Software Services Pvt. Ltd.
Printer/Binder: Courier/Stoughton
Cover Printer: Courier/Stoughton
Text Font: Times New Roman

Library of Congress Cataloging-in-Publication Data

Pelz, William A.
  Karl Marx : a world to win / William A. Pelz.
    p. cm. — (The library of world biography)
  Includes bibliographical references and index.
  ISBN-13: 978-0-321-35583-6 (alk. paper)
  ISBN-10: 0-321-35583-0 (alk. paper)
  1. Marx, Karl, 1818-1883. 2. Socialists—Biography. 3. Socialism—History.
  4. Industrial revolution. I. Title. II. Series.
HX39.5.P384 2012
335.4092—dc22
[B]

2010054526

Prentice Hall
is an imprint of

10 9 8 7 6 5 4 3 2 1

www.pearsonhighered.com

ISBN 13: 978-0-321-35583-6
ISBN 10:   0-321-35583-0

Contents

Editor's Preface

Biography is history seen through the prism of a person.

LOUIS FISCHER

It is often challenging to identify the roles and experiences of individuals in world history. Larger forces predominate. Yet, biography provides important access to world history. It shows how individuals helped shape the society around them. Biography also offers concrete illustrations of larger patterns in political and intellectual life, in family life, and in the economy.

The Library of World Biography series seeks to capture the individuality and drama that mark human character. It deals with individuals operating in one of the main periods of world history, while also reflecting issues in the particular society around them. Here, the individual illustrates larger themes of time and place. The interplay between the personal and general is always the key to using biography in history, and world history is no exception. Always, too, there is the question of personal agency: How much do individuals, even great ones, shape their own lives and environment, and how much are they shaped by the world around them?

PETER N. STEARNS

Author's Preface

History is an unpredictable chameleon revealing different faces to different people at different times—one that is not accorded the attention that it deserves. The same individual who would be horrified by an unqualified person performing a surgery has no problem pontificating on historical matters with their only evidence being a dimly remembered show from the History Channel.

Some historical actors are fated to have their legacy enter into the area of popular culture. Thus, many people think they know about Catherine the Great, George Washington, King Henry VIII, Genghis Khan, or Nelson Mandela. The problem is that what many individuals think they know about history is partial, incomplete, exaggerated, or simply untrue. George Washington may or may not have had a tendency to attack fruit-bearing trees with an ax or throw perfectly good money across rivers. In any case, his importance to the birth of the American Republic has no connection to either fable. That Washington freed his slaves upon his death is significant; whether his false teeth were made of wood or ivory is not. It is a fact that Henry VIII had six wives, but most historians would argue that this fact about his personal life was not his major contribution to world history.

So it is with Karl Marx. So many people "know" so much about him. Frequently, I request that my undergraduate students respond to the question "tell me something about Karl Marx." Surprisingly often, one will respond with great assurance: "He was a Russian." Upon further investigation, it normally turns out that this piece of misinformation came to the unsuspecting student in high school or another college class. This might sound unusual but on more than one occasion, the present author has heard university *history* professors point to Marx as a Russian. That the Russians would later claim Marx as one of their own may be true but in no way changes his actual birth in the western part of Germany in 1818.

One common piece of accepted wisdom is that Marx was an angry loner whom no one, save Engels, could stand to be around. While he was no doubt a difficult individual, particularly to those who had conflicting ideas, this portrait of Marx as an antisocial eccentric is contradicted by numerous contemporary accounts even by police agents and political opponents. Marx opened his home and family to numerous exiles and displaced radicals, including a fair number who disagreed with him and Engels. He may have had sharp political arguments with many, if not most, of these, but the point remains that these individuals remained part of Marx's extended family. This has been convincingly demonstrated in Katherine Hollander's "At Home with the Marxes" article in the March 2010 issue of the *Journal of the Historical Society*.

Famous historical figures are often blamed for events taking place long after their death. Some time ago, Joseph Schumpeter remarked that there is as little in common between Marx and Stalinism as there was between Christ and the Inquisition. Likewise, few rational people would blame St. Paul for current scandals in the Roman Catholic Church but somehow it is still intellectually respectable to make Marx responsible for anything from Mid East dictatorships to the national debt of Greece. Of course, self-proclaimed "Marxists" often invoke his name to justify their own political projects. While some genuinely attempt to apply Marx's methods, many would cause Marx, were he alive today, to again mutter: "All I know is that I'm not a Marxist." Not being a Marxist would appear to be a wise position for Karl Marx to take in a world where even a pope, the archbishop of Canterbury, or a French prime minister has been known to quote Marx when it serves their purpose.

Karl Marx was a pivotal figure in world history who should be understood within his historical context. Mindless praise or violent demonization is not merely unfair; it is ahistorical. Marx must be understood as a person of his time and place in history. The world Karl Marx lived in was one of tremendous, and rapid, socio-economic change. During his life, the seemingly impossible happened, as first the long fragmented parts of Italy united into a nation and then a host of religiously and politically diverse German-speaking lands in Central Europe were hammered together into a united Germany.

Significantly, Marx was born into a Europe, and a world, where the "Rights of Man" were little more than a slogan left over from the French Revolution of 1789. Throughout his life, he witnessed the slow, uneven, but steady growth of democracy. While women remained excluded from voting, an increasing number of adult males were able to win the right to vote. Men who were barely considered citizens in Marx's youth were members of various parliaments by the time of Marx's death. Slavery had been an accepted institution within the Western capitalist world in Marx's youth. By the end of his days, slavery had been outlawed most everywhere and was by then widely considered the moral outrage it was.

He was an eyewitness to the blinding light of industrialization as it swept first Great Britain, then Western Europe, and moved outward to the colonial and semi-colonial worlds. As industrial capitalism triumphed, it unleashed a torrent of technological change and innovation seldom if ever seen before. For the average person, this was accompanied by fierce exploitation as commoners lost their lands and livelihoods as skilled workers. Task-work discipline that allowed personal autonomy as long as the needed task was completed when needed (e.g., the harvest brought in) was replaced by time-work discipline. That is, the common people were increasingly forced to sell their time along with their labor, losing control over both.

In this whirlwind of change, it was easy to adopt a simple response. Some condemned the Industrial Revolution as an inhuman disaster that must be reversed. Others thought the very real human cost of the new system irrelevant or a necessary sacrifice on the altar of progress. It was the genius of Marx to understand that industrialization was a great step forward in human history, but it would only benefit the average person if its abuses were curbed and its benefits distributed to everyone. His nuanced, dialectical, approach marks Marx as a thinker towering above his more one-dimensional counterparts.

Hopefully, this work will impart some sense of who Karl Marx was and why he still matters. This work is far from complete or comprehensive. Books have been written about Karl Marx and his work that run up to five hundred pages, if not longer. In far fewer pages, this work seeks to introduce the novice to Marx and allows her or him to decide whether they wish to delve deeper.

As is always the case, this book has profited from the advice and help of more people than this writer can ever properly thank. Rob DeGeorge at Pearson deserves special thanks for his patience with the author's delays and refusal to listen to what was probably very good advice. Throughout the writing process, Adrienne Butler helped me make sense of my ideas. John Metz had countless useful suggestions that have improved this work. My ideas were sharpened by discussions with other intellectuals including but not limited to: Eric Schuster, Truman College; Axel Fair-Schultz, SUNY-Potsdam; Peter Hudis, Loyola University; Ottokar Luban (Berlin); Bryan Palmer (Toronto); Francis King (England); Steven McGiffen (France); Narihito Ito (Tokyo); Sobhanlal Datta Gupta (Calcutta); Theo Bergmann (Stuttgart); Bruno Drwenski (Paris); Ronald van Raak (Amsterdam); Mario Kessler (Berlin); Lea Haro (Glasgow); and Jean-Pierre Page (Havana). Many, many thanks go to students who have read drafts and provided vital translation skills so that the book is written in twenty-first-century English, while their proofreading often caught errors that older eyes had missed: Olivia Happel, Hayley Jackson, Jean Panichi, and Kate Alonzo.

The following reviewers provided helpful suggestions throughout the process of writing and revising the manuscript: Charles A. Endress, Angelo State University; Joseph T. Fuhrmann, Murray State University; Ann R. Higginbotham, Eastern Connecticut State University; John Monroe, Iowa State University; Henry Reichman, California State University; William S. Rodner, Tidewater Community College; Steven C. Rubert, Oregon State University; Charles M. Sherrod, Albany State University; David Stone, Kansas State University; and Robert Strayer, California State University at Monterey Bay.

Naturally, any errors or omissions in either fact or interpretation are no reflection on any of the people listed above. They are in fact the responsibility of my cat, Nicki, who agreed that I could blame him. Like Marx, he, too, is not Russian.

WILLIAM A. PELZ

Introduction

Is Marx Dead?

How can one describe Karl Marx? To call him a philosopher or political activist is accurate but such a characterization suffers from understatement, as much as saying the Grand Canyon is a ditch in the western United States. Moreover, a radical thinker and activist who lived in the nineteenth century would, at first, seem to be at best a footnote in history. After all, Marx never lived to see any successful socialist revolutions. Many who built socialist states in the twentieth century and claimed to be "Marxist" would likely have elicited Marx's criticism, if not outright scorn. As an individual dedicated to democracy, only the most jaundiced observer could claim that Marx would have applauded such human tragedies as Stalin's Russia or the hermit kingdom of North Korea.

Though often misinterpreted and misrepresented, the man from Trier is far from insignificant. In 1983, on the hundredth anniversary of Marx's death, an iconic poster issued by the French Communist Party, part of the governing coalition at that time, had his portrait with the caption: "Marx is dead." In response, Marx mockingly points to his open eye while saying "my eye." Time after time, people have pronounced Marx "dead" only to witness a rebirth of interest in his ideas. One is reminded of the reaction of French King Louis Philippe who exclaimed, on being told of the death of Napoleon's famous and devious former diplomat Talleyrand, "What did he mean by that?" Scholars, not to mention average people, have had the same reaction to much of what concerns Marx. What ideas remain relevant from this long-dead German revolutionary? Naturally, there is a spectrum of answers to this question, and the exploration of some will demonstrate Marx's historical impact.

One inevitably encounters difficulty in any attempt to fairly evaluate Marx's impact on history, politics, and society. Since his death, Marx has been treated alternatively as god or devil, depending upon one's political leanings. This meant that the real historical Marx was lost because, as Ernesto Che Guervara complained, "St. Marx" had been distorted and "turned into a stone idol." For others, Marx was the font of all evil in the contemporary world. British historian Robert Service blamed Marx, who lived in the nineteenth century, for most of what went wrong in the twentieth century. Service managed to blame Marx for not only Stalin but also Hitler and Saddam Hussein. Marx, being dead, was

1

unable to defend himself from such specious associations. In contrast, noted author John Berger asks how "is it possible not to heed Marx, who prophesied and analyzed the devastation [caused by capitalism]?"

Marx continues to have a presence in popular culture and has literary defenders. Award-winning mystery writer Berry Maitland set one of his first novels in London amidst a group of fictional descendants of the German exile. Although in most ways a conventional (yet still well written) British whodunit, Maitland ends with a speech by one of Marx's mythical great-granddaughters. Arguing that his work was misunderstood and misrepresented, the fictional descendant maintains that Marx's work would be vindicated in the future. Stating that he understood the impossibility of socialism in backward peasant nations, she continues that "he understood that it was only by passing through the complete cycle of capitalist development that a society would experience its inner contradictions to the full, and thus be capable [of achieving] true socialism."

In order to analyze Marx, an author faces a task much like that of the nineteenth-century historian Thomas Carlyle while writing about Oliver Cromwell, the leader of the English Revolution of the seventeenth century. Carlyle wrote that doing justice to Cromwell involved first exhuming his body out "from under a heap of dead dogs." From under dictators who have falsely claimed Marx's heritage and reactionaries eager to pin all the worlds' sorrows on him, Marx too has to be revived.

In a perverse way, the volume of abuse and false praise Marx has generated is a tribute to the once-obscure German intellectual who daily dragged himself to the reading room of the British Museum. There, he conducted factual research upon which he would base his theories. If his life and work had been without significant impact, it would be meaningless to recast the all-too-human Marx as an important historical figure. As he himself freely admitted, Marx was a product of his time and place in history. He was fond of saying that people make history, but not in the conditions or time of their own choosing. What makes Marx noteworthy was his ability to look beyond the immediate realities and envision future possibilities.

An unusually striking instance of this ability is his often-cited description of the emergence of a global market. While rampant nationalism blinded many to the ever more global nature of society, Marx was able to see a tendency toward globalization as early as the middle of the nineteenth century. Meanwhile, as many of his contemporaries confidently predicted a future of peace and prosperity—an "end of history"—Marx saw that the contradictions of society were leading to war and depression. This was not because Marx was clairvoyant, but because he embraced new ideas as changes in reality dictated, that is something many writers and observers hesitate to do both now and then.

Marx's Ongoing Influence

Marx remains an important thinker, even as his once-famous contemporaries have faded into obscurity. In 2005, a British Broadcasting Corporation (BBC) radio's poll of listeners found Marx to be "history's greatest philosopher," despite campaigns by *The Economist* and *The Financial Times* to promote Adam Smith and then, in desperation, David Hume. The same year, the German weekly *Der Spiegel* put him on their cover with the title "A Spectre is back." In a curious and little reported incident in October 2007, Marx's name came up during a talk to 5,000 New York businessmen by Alan Greenspan. The former head of the US Federal Reserve caused murmurs of disbelief when he noted that the egalitarianism Marx supported could "be a solution to today's income inequality." Since the start of the economic crisis during the latter part of 2008, more and more references have been made to Marx and his work, including billionaire George Soros stating, "I've been reading Marx and there is an awful lot in what he says."

Best-selling American author Barbara Ehrenreich, in an op-ed piece in the *Chicago Sun-Times,* joked that 2008 was the 160th anniversary of the *Communist Manifesto*, and the international bourgeoisie had decided to commemorate the event by collapsing world capitalism. On October 4, 2008, the British business weekly *The Economist* contained a color portrait of mainstream conservative French President Sarkozy eagerly reading Marx's *Das Kapital* and quoted him as declaring, "Laissez-faire [free-market capitalism] is finished." By April 2009, the *Financial Times* was even claiming that now the French President "likes to be photographed clutching a copy of *Das Kapital*."

By the end of 2008, Britain's *Guardian* had reported that "Karl Marx is back," while Berlin's Dietz Publishing's sales of Marx's writings have soared 300 percent. This was not simply the result of the proletariat looking for answers as the German economy began to deteriorate, since even the federal German finance minister admitted to *Spiegel* that "certain parts of Marx's theory are really not so bad."

The Irish Times noted that since the 2008 economic crisis Marx "has suddenly become popular again." In London, a center of the capitalist system, readers of *The Times* were asked in a poll if Marx "had got it right." By late October, over half answered in the affirmative. "Karl Marx was never so right as now," claimed Portugal's only Nobel laureate Jose Saramago in late 2008. The influence in fiction continued as *Das Kapital: A Novel of Love and Money Markets* was published in French in early 2009. This homage to Marx includes a professor at the New School in New York who is reduced to driving a taxi. This drop in lifestyle does nothing to alter the character's views, as he explains to a passenger how "the fundamental truth Marx grasped early and chose to grasp as a tragedy. We sell the time of our lives for wages. It's not just that time is money. It's that life, which is energy exercised over time, is exchanged for money. Life is money; energy is money; time is money. Money is the universal solvent . . ."

If the March 20, 2009, *New York Times* is correct, Marx's work will venture into what well may be a new medium. The newspaper reported that Chinese Opera director He Nian wrote an adaptation of *Das Kapital* that was performed in Shanghai in 2010. Somewhat unexpected was the report in the April 2009 issue of *Le Monde diplomatique* on sales in Germany of Marx's *Das Kapital* but not that Marx or that *Das Kapital.* Reinhard Marx, a former bishop in Karl Marx's birthplace of Trier and now archbishop of Munich, shares more than merely the famous last name. Choosing to name his book on Roman Catholic social doctrine after Karl Marx's economic opus, Archbishop Marx writes in the preface to "dear Karl Marx." After telling the older Marx that "he was not completely wrong," the archbishop argues that society must be reformed so Marx can "rest in peace." Not that the good archbishop is a socialist. He argues "if we do not meet the challenges of our time, Karl Marx will return from the grave, and that must not happen." In the same year, Rowan Williams, the archbishop of Canterbury, has repeated spoken out in defense of many of Karl Marx's ideas and even Pope Benedict XVI has spoken of Marx's "great analytical skill."

Jean-Marie Harribey, a French economist, has noted that the business press, from the *Financial Times* and the *Economist* to the *Wall Street Journal,* has all admitted Marx's relevance by the end of 2008. Harribey observed that "one might draw up an impressive list of publications at the service of capitalistic interests that draw upon Marx's critique of capitalism to try and find their way through the erratic movements of their own system." In 2009, *The Atlantic Times* business section commented: "The writings of Karl Marx long consigned to the dustbin of history, have taken on a new relevance . . . In grasping capitalism's susceptibility to crisis; Marx was right on the money."

While still vilified by many, Marx has been accepted as one of the classic critics of industrial capitalism. Many times Marx, as well as his ideas, has been declared dead. After the people who made these pronouncements were long forgotten, a new generation decides to have another look at Marx. Although this could be a form of nostalgia, it could be because, as historian Eric Hobsbawm argued in 2008, "Marx remains a superb guide to understanding the world and the problems we must confront." Maybe Alain Minc, successful businessman and good friend of the conservative French President, said it best: "If Marx imposes himself as one of the 'unsurpassable' thinkers of our time, the reason is . . . mostly, that he was the first to detect the dynamics intrinsic to capitalism." Of course, it could be that Archbishop Marx is right about the socialist Marx. If capitalism fails to change, Dr. Marx, or more accurately his ideas, will return from the grave.

1

Marx before the *Manifesto*

Introduction

On May 5, 1818, little noticed outside their circle of family and friends, Henriette Marx gave birth to a son, Karl. While his lawyer father, Heinrich Marx, was doubtless happy at Karl's arrival, he had no idea his son would one day become famous, or to his enemies, infamous. Karl Marx was born in Trier in the western part of what would one day become Germany but was then a collection of small, disunited kingdoms and principalities. Coming on the German scene shortly after the defeat of Napoleon and the earlier French Revolution, Karl Marx would grow up in a contradictory environment. On the one hand, Trier was part of Prussia, a militaristic and conservative kingdom that was allied to the Russian Tsar. Yet, Trier was an ancient city dating back to the Romans that was deeply influenced by the decades of revolution and liberalism washing over from France, her neighbor to the west. Later, in *The Eighteenth Brumaire of Louis Bonaparte*, Marx waxed enthusiastically about how "beyond the French frontier, he [Napoleon Bonaparte] swept away everywhere the establishments of feudalism, so far as requisite, to furnish the bourgeois social system of France with fit surroundings of the European continent."

Within the Marx Family

On the surface, the Marx family was respectably Protestant, solidly in the Prussian upper middle class. However, Heinrich and Henriette Marx had been Jews who converted to Christianity to avoid the stifling anti-Semitism of their day. As reaction swept through Prussia in the wake of Napoleon's defeat in 1815, Jews were excluded from all public office, the legal profession, and even running drug stores. The fact that Marx's grandfather was a rabbi must have had at least an indirect effect on the younger Marx. On his mother's side of the family, there were also rabbis, although Marx's uncle Philips would be the grandfather of the founder of the Philips' Electronics cartel. One wonders what the revolutionary Karl Marx would make of his mother's relatives cranking out plasma televisions to the masses in the twenty-first century. Despite their conversion, to many the Marxes and their son, baptized a Lutheran in 1824, remained somehow Jewish. Thus Karl Marx is often referred to as a "Jew" yet seldom called a "Lutheran."

While always proud of their son's towering intellect, Marx's parents were often deeply frustrated by his lack of interest in a conventional career. For instance, his mother is reported to have once sighed, "If only Karl had made Capital, instead of written it." Still, Heinrich Marx was no uncultured social climber who converted solely to continue his legal career. He had read works by such radical Enlightenment philosophers as Voltaire, Rousseau, and Kant. Heinrich had liberal and oppositional tendencies—a relative rarity in a conservative and conformist state. The elder Marx was nonetheless no radical but rather a moderate who remained loyal to the Prussian monarchy even while voicing some pointed criticisms. Karl Marx seemed deeply attached to his father. According to his daughter Eleanor, Marx talked frequently about Heinrich and always carried an old photograph of his father.

Marx as Student

For five years, Karl Marx attended Friedrich-Wilhelm Gymnasium, a Jesuit school in Trier. There he began to learn history from Principal Wyttenbach, who was known throughout the Rhineland as a liberal with a reputation for unusual ideas in the field of philosophy. Wyttenbach may well have had an influence on the young Marx. While his formal academic achievement was only average, Marx learned much about the world of ideas outside his province from his father as well as his future father-in-law, Privy Councilor Ludwig von Westphalen. His father read French classics with him, while the latter introduced Marx to the ideas of the French socialist Saint-Simon. When he graduated in September 1835 at the age of seventeen, the Royal Examination Commission stated that Marx was "gifted and showed a very commendable industry in old languages, in German and in history, a commendable industry in mathematics and only a limited industry in French."

Bowing to his father's wish that he study law, Marx left Trier in mid-October 1835. He traveled by boat to Bonn, which was little bigger than Trier and dominated by the university and its seven hundred students, as it had become the intellectual center for the Prussian Rhineland. The French July Revolution in the beginning of the 1830s had given progressive Germans hope that the feudal system, which had predominated since the Middle Ages with hereditary aristocrats monopolizing all power in their hands, might soon be overthrown. Unlike England, a completely capitalist society that was in the early stages of the Industrial Revolution, or France with their revolutionary tradition of "liberty, equality, fraternity," all the German states, to one degree or another, still labored under feudal restrictions left over from the Middle Ages.

Fearing that the winds of liberty generated in the west would blow away the ancient feudal system of nobles, kings, and the church, the German states everywhere instituted widespread repression. Thousands of radicals were imprisoned or driven into exile. Some of these were believers in the republican form of government (republicans no relation to current political parties) who wished to see an end to the rule of kings, princes, and dukes. Others held out for democracy (democrats no relation to current parties), and believed that at least a portion of the citizenry, usually who were male and affluent, should be allowed to elect governmental officials. As part of the campaign of repression, newspapers were banned and all political associations outlawed. Even wearing the national democratic colors of black, red, and gold became a criminal offense.

At the university, the young Marx was not directly involved in political activity instead he joined an association of progressive young poets. He and his friends often traded insults or punches with the sons of Junkers, the feudal lords of Prussia. In what even he later realized was a throwback to an earlier era, Marx went so far as to fight a duel with one unduly arrogant offspring of the aristocracy in the summer of 1836. The contradictions within Marx are apparent even at this time of his life. On the one hand, he was interested in new ideas and social change, yet at many times in his personal life, he was very much a man of conventional behavior.

As the dueling incident suggests, it would be a mistake to think of Marx as simply an overly serious scholar who spent all his time poring over dry manuscripts while at Bonn University. The reality was that Marx and his friends devoted a great deal of time to drinking bouts accompanied by riotous singing so much so that, in June of 1836, the university administration sentenced him to a day of detention for being drunken and disorderly one night. During his admittedly lenient confinement, he was visited by a number of his buddies. Instead of quietly discussing their academic work, things got out of hand once more and Marx received still further detention. All of this proved too much for a worried Heinrich Marx, who informed the Bonn University authorities that the younger Marx would transfer to Berlin University in the autumn.

Karl Marx's Love of Jenny von Westphalen

Setting out for Berlin in October 1836, Marx soon found himself, not in another college town like Bonn, but in a large city of 300,000 residents. He left behind more than his family and college friends. By late summer 1836, Marx had clearly fallen in love with Jenny von Westphalen, the daughter of an important local aristocratic family. Not only her father was a Prussian baron, but also her mother was a descendent of Scottish nobility. Marx wrote poetry to his intelligent and cultured future wife. In 1837, the future author of such decidedly unromantic works as *Theories of Surplus Value* wrote,

> Jenny! Teasingly you may inquire
> Why my songs "To Jenny" I address,
> When for you alone my pulse beats higher,
> When my songs for you alone despair,
> When you only can their heart inspire,
> When your name each syllable must confess,
> When you lend each note melodiousness,
> When no breath would stray from the Goddess?

At first glance, the social distance between the two young people would have appeared to doom the match. Still, his affection was returned and the couple became secretly engaged. Marx, a lawyer's son from a family of Jewish descent, had become engaged to a daughter of the noble von Westphalen family. This was very unusual for early nineteenth-century Central Europe, which was still in the grip of traditional feudal prejudice against "commoners," let alone "Jews." Of course, Marx had to convince his own family as well.

In a surviving letter to his father written in 1837 after his arrival in Berlin, we get a glimpse of Karl Marx's relentless campaign. At one point, he argued how everything left him cold as "no work of art was as beautiful as Jenny." After discussing his studies, wishing his family speedy recover from their illness, he again returned to his personal feelings. The last lines asked his father to say hello to "my sweet, wonderful Jenny. I have read her letter twelve times already, and always discover new delights in it. It is in every respect, including that of style, the most beautiful letter I can imagine being written by a woman."

Ultimately won over despite his misgivings, Heinrich Marx agreed to smooth the way with Jenny's parents. In the end, the von Westphalen family agreed. Despite this, they would not marry until after Marx had received his doctorate and the death of his father—the better part of a decade. On June 19, 1843, the couple was married, with the only guests being Jenny's mother and her brother Edgar, along with a few friends. They would remain together until death, suffering through poverty, illness, and the premature death of a number of children. The evidence confirms what their friends always said: They were deeply in love with each other. All the same, like many other men, Marx was at least partially mystified by what those in the nineteenth century called the weaker sex. "Women, even when gifted with understanding," he privately wrote to Frederick Engels, "are curious creatures." In holding to this attitude, he revealed that for all his pronounced radicalism, Karl Marx continued clinging to many of the male prejudices of his age. For all his radical belief in the socialist future, his own marriage would, in most ways, prove to be a conventional bourgeois marriage.

In the Realm of Philosophy

Marx's academic focus at Berlin University soon drifted from law to philosophy. Berlin had been home to important German philosophers like Kant, Fichte, and most of all Hegel. At the time of his death in 1831, Hegel was likely the most influential thinker in Central Europe. His books were widely read and he had attracted an impressive following. Marx's beliefs, following the path of Hegel, centered on the use of a philosophical method known as dialectics. By the age of nineteen, he wrote to his father telling him he had reached a turning point in his life. In that letter, dated November 1837, he explains his conversion to the conflict-based theories of Hegelian philosophy and the dialectical method with the clear encouragement of a number of his professors. This philosophy was not only idealistic, in that it concentrated on the power of ideas rather than material forces, but it was also conservative and used to justify the monarchical Prussian state.

The concept of dialectics comes primarily from the ancient Greek thinker Heraclittus. One important aspect of this theory is that everything is in a state of constant change. You cannot step in the same river twice because the river is always in motion. In the modern era, it was Hegel who took this method as the basis for his philosophical system. Typically, modern dialectics are presented as arguing that out of today's world (thesis) grows oppositional forces (antitheses). Out of this conflict between the two grows a synthesis. This synthesis in turn gives rise to a new antithesis ultimately resulting in another synthesis. This popular, but overly simplistic, view ignores that Hegel always saw contradictions as inherent in and internal to each thesis, rather than the synthesis. That is, change comes through conflict but that conflict is already present within each thesis. For Hegel, this dialectical process was based on the conflict and evolution of ideas.

It was said later that Marx turned Hegel on his head, since Marx saw dialectical conflicts as emerging from material forces, not abstract ideas. Marx's *Capital* is written with the view that history moves because of material contradictions. In other words, such things as the relation between various social classes, the manner that products are produced, who owns the means of production are all factors in moving history forward. In the thought of Marx (and Engels), the essence of dialectics is the concept of class struggle playing the leading role. Thus, as both argue in their *Communist Manifesto*, all history is the history of class struggles. If Hegel saw the conflict between ideas as creating the motion of history, then Marx saw it as the war between social classes.

Each historical epoch has within it contradictions. For example, Slave society had the contradiction between master and slaves. During the Middle Ages, feudal society contained the struggle between lord and serf. In the modern world, Marx saw the contradiction as being between capitalists—who wanted the lowest possible labor costs—and workers—who wanted a higher standard of living. Marx was in many ways the opposite of Hegel, since the latter believed that ideas created material reality. For Marx, the material world gave rise to certain types of ideas. In his words, "being determines consciousness," maybe a play-off of Descartes "I think, and therefore, I am."

Young Hegelians

After Hegel's demise, those who embraced his philosophy very quickly split into two mutually hostile camps. On one side stood most of Hegel's older and more conservative students who supported interpretations supportive of the status quo. These people would point to the fact that their conclusions were essentially the same as those of Hegel himself—especially late in life. In opposition arose a leftist group who, on account of their generally more youthful supporters, became known as the "Young Hegelians." Their most common theme was the need to use Hegel's dialectical method to mount radical critiques of religion, society, and politics. If the old (right-wing) Hegelians argued that philosophy had basically ended with the death of their master, the young (left-wing) Hegelians were intent on "applying Hegel to Hegel."

The radical Young Hegelians included many notable philosophers like Bruno Bauer, Arnold Ruge, and Ludwig Feuerbach. Notably, Feuerbach took Hegel's idea that God created people in order to be truly God and turned it around: He argued people created a god who had qualities humans lacked. Ultimately, most of these young scholars became atheistic in their religious views. Important in the 1830s and 1840s, the Young Hegelian group originally attracted both Marx and Engels to their circle.

By the end of the 1830s, those thinkers known as the Young Hegelians claimed Hegel and the dialectic method for revolution. This was an open challenge to the traditional Hegelians who were idealistic supporters of the reactionary Prussian state. The former believed that the method of Hegel could be used to disprove that the Prussian state was the historic "realization of the Absolute Idea" or what today might be called the end of history. Recovering from illness during the summer of 1837, Marx had worked his way through Hegel's writings. A college friend introduced Marx to a group of Young Hegelians known as the *Doktorklub*, whose members included Bruno Bauer and Arnold Ruge. This group met regularly at a Berlin café, spending hours in heated—and often drunken—intellectual disputes. Although he later had heated disagreements with many of his fellows and he was younger than most members, Marx would remain with the club until graduation in 1841.

Marx began to feel constrained by the limits of mainstream Hegelian thinking, while retaining some of the more radical elements of Hegelian philosophy.

By the early 1840s, the young intellectual came to believe the problem was with Hegel, and the Young Hegelians—namely their obsessive focus on ideas over material realities. Examining the American and French revolutions, Marx argued that both stressed formal political liberty while ignoring the need for social or human emancipation. Both he and Engels would later break with the Young Hegelians in a biting attack entitled *The Holy Family* (1844). In 1845, in his *Theses on Feuerbach,* Marx would make his oft quoted remark: "Philosophers have only interpreted the world in various ways. The point is, however, to change it."

While at Berlin University, Marx was typically in debt, a situation made worse with the death of his father on May 10, 1838. Exempted from military service because of chest "weakness," the young intellectual rushed to finish his PhD dissertation in hopes of getting a university teaching job, and thus a source of income. By the time he finished the dissertation, Berlin University saw academic freedom extinguished by Friedrich Wilhelm IV, who became king in 1840. Academic freedom and the right to one's own ideas had once been respected, and now everyone was expected to follow the politics promoted by the King's government. So Marx sent his dissertation to Jena University, known for its easy-going attitude toward intellectual matters. Thus, only little more than a week after his dissertation was submitted, on April 15, 1841, Marx was awarded his PhD.

Returning to Trier, Karl Marx planned to embark on the honorable, if normally obscure, career of a college professor. Traveling to Bonn in July 1841, the newly minted *doctor* visited his friend Bruno Bauer, who worked as a lecturer at the university. Had Dr. Marx been able to get a comfortable university post, would his role in history have changed? It is impossible to say. In any event, the wave of reaction that washed over Berlin University soon reached the Bonn campus, and Bruno Bauer found himself driven out of the university. The end of Bauer's career at Bonn was a sign of the purging of critical thinkers from academia and thus, at the same time, the death of Marx's dream of a university post. The young Dr. Marx would now turn to political journalism.

From the Halls of Academia to the Shores of Political Journalism

His first turn at journalism was an attack on a new censorship law, written while visiting his gravely ill would-be father-in-law, Baron von Westphalen, in Trier in February 1842. Ridiculing various proposed reforms, Marx wrote the "only genuine cure for the censorship would be its abolition." The censors immediately banned Marx's piece. Naturally enough, this merely confirmed in Marx's mind the evils of the old order and its restriction on the free flow of ideas. In May 1842, in his first contribution to the newspaper *Rheinische Zeitung*, he attacked not only Prussian absolutism—the idea that all power emanated from the imperial throne, regardless of the ability of the person seated upon it—but also bourgeois liberals who would turn the press into a mere source of profit. "The first freedom of the press," Marx argued, is "to be free of commerce." Despite this decidedly unfriendly attitude toward business, the paper's shareholders made Marx editor in mid-October. While only twenty-four years old, Marx had emerged as the leading voice of progressive businessmen and professionals.

Marx's appointment was further cause for the pro-big business and national liberal *Allgemeine Zeitung* to attack the *Rheinische Zeitung* as an institution of Prussian Communism. As editor, Marx replied that they did not even admit that "communist ideas in their present form possess even theoretical reality, and therefore can still less desire their practical realization." Marx may have had one eye on the censors when he made this relatively neutral statement, but it is also true he felt his knowledge of socialism and communism was still sparse and as yet inadequate.

When a new law was proposed that would make it a crime for the poor to continue their ancient custom of collecting fallen wood, Marx was compelled to compose his first piece on a social question. At the beginning of 1843, he undertook an investigation of the plight of peasants in the Moselle region, who possessed tiny vineyards. Discovering that the winemakers were unable to compete with cheap imported wine from elsewhere in Germany, the *Rheinische Zeitung* accused the government of indifference to the legitimate complaints of these impoverished peasants. The Prussian government reacted angrily, charging the paper with slander and demanding retractions. On January 21, 1843, Berlin issued an edict revoking the *Rheinische Zeitung*'s publishing license as of March 31. It later turned out that the direct cause was actually a request from the Russian Tsar, offended by what the divine-right ruler thought was an anti-Russian article.

Realizing that his effectiveness as editor was at an end, the twenty-four year-old resigned on March 18, blaming the "present censorship situation." His editorship was by no means a failure, as his spirited articles had drawn readers to the paper. When he began as editor, the *Rheinische Zeitung* had 885 paid subscribers, whereas three months later it had 3,400 subscribers. The experience would also have an important impact on the young doctor of philosophy. Marx began to think about the significance of social and material interests in human society. This reflection led Marx to question the usefulness of a purely idealistic philosophy detached from political action.

More personally, he saw his struggle with the Prussian censors as an indication of the moral rot of the old feudal establishment. Declaring he could never feel free in a Germany dominated by feudal lords and militarists, Karl Marx resolved to leave the home of his birth. There was, however, still the matter of his long-suffering fiancée Jenny, who had waited for him for seven years. Jenny had to endure almost a decade of abuse from her reactionary and aristocratic relatives, who could not understand her pledge to a broke subversive. Still, on June 19, 1843, in the spa resort of Kreuznach, Dr. Karl Marx wed Jenny von Westphalen with her mother, her brother Edgar, and a few friends as witnesses. Interestingly enough, none of Marx's relatives attended.

Exile in Paris

After a brief honeymoon, Jenny and Karl Marx moved to Paris in October 1843. Moving into a modest building on the left bank of the River Seine where other leftist German emigrants lived, Marx commenced work on a new journal, *The German-French Yearbook*, with Arnold Ruge. One of the first people he asked to contribute was Ludwig Feuerbach, who had been the first to argue that being determines thought. Feuerbach believed in keeping his insight purely within the field of philosophy, while the young Marx thought theory and practice needed to be combined.

Living in Paris was an important, maybe transformative, experience for the young German radical and his wife. In France, they lived in a world where capitalism ruled and the Industrial Revolution was starting to replace hand labor with machines, as it had already done in England. France was the product of the great Revolution of 1789 and the lesser one of 1830. Unlike the stress on obedience common in German lands, liberal France proclaimed the ideals of "liberty, fraternity, equality." All of this made Paris a hotbed of radicals and revolutionaries from throughout Europe and the place where socialist ideas most widely circulated. Not surprisingly, Marx found this environment both new and stimulating.

In the middle of the nineteenth century, France may have been the mother of revolution, but it was also a capitalist society with a small growing working class. This new social group, slowly multiplying through industrialization, captured the German exile's attention. Coming from a land as of yet little touched by the revolution in production, Marx at first knew little about this emerging industrial proletariat. He was able to see that the way things had been produced for centuries, by hand, was being replaced by the mechanized production of goods. These machines were owned by capitalists who prospered from their ever constant improvement, while the traditional worker's tools became obsolete. With neither sufficient capital nor skills required by the new machinery, these workers accepted lower paying jobs in factories in order to survive. Convinced that the industrial capitalism so firmly established in England and growing in France would soon sweep over Europe and ultimately the world, Karl Marx resolved to study this new world of capital and industry. During the summer of 1844, he threw himself into an examination of British political economy. Marx set out on a systematic study of the works of economists like Adam Smith, David Ricardo, and James Mill. Still, his public writings of the mid-1840s were marked by the philosophical approach one would expect from a German *Herr Doktor*. He was, in a phrase, still involved in abstract theoretical formulations rather than concrete examples and thoughts.

Meanwhile, the would-be revolutionary had more immediate matters demanding his attention. Jenny was, as they said in those days, with child. On the first of May 1844, Jenny gave birth to a baby daughter named after her, but more often called "Jennychen" by her parents. The new parents had one problem after another with their new baby, arguably through a mixture of bad luck and inexperience at parenting. By June, Jenny and her daughter retreated home to her mother, Baroness von Westphalen, in Trier. With medical care, a wet nurse, and some tender loving, Marx's daughter survived the perils of early infancy.

The German-French Yearbook did not fare as well. Despite living in a city that may have contained more writers per capita than any other on the planet, few French authors agreed to contribute to the journal. Marx was soon feuding with his main collaborator, Ruge, who quickly withdrew from the entire project, thereby leading to its demise. Additionally, many copies were confiscated en masse by police in Prussia, Bavaria, the Austrian Empire, and elsewhere. The message that Europe could live and prosper without being ruled over by hereditary monarchies and that maybe a democracy of some sort would be a better alternative never reached those it was aimed at. Although the police repression may have been a tribute to the radical message of the journal, it hardly made the project a financial success. Of course, as his mother had noted, making money was not her son's strong suit. Plunging into financial destitution, the Marx family was saved by the timely donation of money from friends and political supporters, including some comrades who paid for a hundred confiscated copies of the *Yearbook*.

Karl Marx and the "Jewish Question"

Around this time, the young Marx was experimenting with his new critical methods and chose to analyze the situation of Jews in *On the Jewish Question*. Attempting to combat Bruno Bauer's view that Jews had to be emancipated from their religion, Marx approached this subject from the viewpoint that it was a social problem. Marx opposed the idea that Jews should be denied civil rights unless they converted to Christianity. Regardless of whatever good intentions he may have had, he clearly wrote things that could easily be misinterpreted as anti-Semitic. Most scholars have concluded that it was more a lacking of understanding Jewish history and culture than being "self-hating" or anti-Semitic. Other people have dismissed this work as more a piece of clumsy philosophizing rather than a sign of anti-Semitism.

All the same, Marx would, throughout his life, refer to Jewish political opponents with negative phrases, if not outright racial slurs. This weakness of Marx may have stemmed from his hostility to the Jewish religion, which he considered tribal and backward, or from a need to distance himself from the maligned group of his ancestors. Karl Marx was a brilliant person, and some would say a genius, yet he was the complicated product of a time when emancipated Jews often looked back on their more traditional and religious colleagues with disgust and revulsion. Like all people, Marx was a person of his time. Perhaps surprisingly or not, his daughter Eleanor was always proud to the point of boastfulness of her Jewish heritage. Yet, Eleanor's father seemed comfortable with, if not proud of, her enthusiasm.

Partnership with Friedrich Engels

Despite attempts to separate and distinguish between the ideas of Marx and his friend, Frederick (or Friedrich) Engels, it is hard to imagine one without the other. Throughout their adult lives, they were intellectual and political partners in what they both saw as an important intellectual and social project. Born to the family of a textile manufacturer in the quickly industrializing Rhineland in 1820, Engels took note of the plight of textile workers at a young age. His father was seemingly without compassion, removing the young Friedrich from school and forcing him to work in the family business. Despite his rejection of his father's ruthless pursuit of profit, Engels was to become an acute and experienced businessman. Engels watched with deep excitement the growth of anti-feudal movements throughout Western Europe. Over time, he grew convinced that only a revolution by the common people would rid Germany of its old feudal lords and welcome in a realm of freedom.

In September 1842, Engels had completed his military service commonly required of young men in most parts of Germany and was headed for England. There he was to become a clerk in the cotton firm of Ermen & Engels, in which his father was a partner. On his way, Engels stopped at the *Rheinische Zeitung* where Marx worked in Cologne. This first meeting with Marx was cool and distant as both had heard unfavorable things about the other. Of greater importance was the visit of Engels to Marx while passing through Paris in August 1844. Engels noted that this meeting left a deep impression on him. Engels stayed in Paris for ten days and spent most of it in discussion with Marx. They found that they shared a broad range of political, economic, and philosophical views. This led the two German radicals to agree to embark on joint projects.

This was to be the start of an intense friendship and historic collaboration. Given that they both traveled in the somewhat limited circles of German radical democrats, their meeting is not surprising. The two men could hardly have appeared more different. Engels was a tall blond Germanic type who was always well dressed. He carried himself with a stiffness that suggested something of the army barracks or at least the business world. Marx was short, dark, and seemingly indifferent to his outward appearance. Engels had a great flair for organization, whereas Marx seemed helpless even in the face of ordering a small household.

From the summer of 1844 onward, it would be increasingly impossible to imagine Marx without Engels any more than Marx could have managed his rather disordered life without his faithful Jenny. Engels' importance for the Marx family was financial as well as intellectual and personal. It was money and gifts from Engels that often saw the Marxes through their recurring bouts of poverty. Beyond his importance financially, Engels would scold Marx if the latter fell behind in his writing. Though Engels dashed off letter after letter telling Marx to complete a given project, the brilliant German *Doktor* would more often than not overlook the well-intended nagging. Without this prodding, Marx might have completed even fewer of his projects.

They shared a deep commitment to radical politics and a genuine sympathy for the oppressed. Still, Marx and Engels were both men of great contradictions. Both had bourgeois lifestyles and resorted to racial insults when describing both ally and enemy alike. If anything, Engels' greater means led to even more apparent contradictions with a lavish lifestyle the workers could only dream of. While Marx was left to petty vanities like sending out party invitations stressing his education and his wife's noble heritage by signing "Dr. Karl Marx and Jenny Marx *nee von Westphalen*," Engels could actually live the life of a bourgeois. A member of the Manchester Stock Exchange, he appeared perfectly respectable to business associates with his frock coat and fine manners. Not only did Engels attend all the obligatory business gatherings, but he also became an avid participant in foxhunts and all manners of upper-class amusement.

Engels, particularly when young, seemed to have a very sexist view of women. One English biographer has gone so far as to suggest that he was a sexual predator in his youth. Unlike Marx, he did not see much in marriage, either in the future or in the present, although he lived for years with an Irish working-class woman. After her death, he became involved with her sister. Karl and Jenny Marx always keep a certain social distance from "Engels' women." As Engels matured, he began to develop into a theorist of socialist feminism as both letters and his famous *Origins of the Family* indicate.

Engels dared not let his conservative parents know of his radical beliefs. He hid them so successfully that into middle age, Engels was able to pass as a typical businessman rather than the revolutionary intellectual he truly was. While attending to the family business, he took time out to investigate the actual living standards of the common people, producing the classic *The Condition of the Working Class in England* in 1845. Investigating slums seldom seen by people of his class, Engels was shocked to see the truly inhuman plight of the average proletarian. Many have argued that with this work, Engels established the basis for a scientific critique of capitalism. In this context, "scientific" is meant as a way of contrasting this approach with the utopian method. That is, Marx and Engels based their theories on the facts as they understood them rather than a series of a priori moral beliefs. Thus, even before his alliance with Marx, Engels was following a parallel path toward socialism and dissent.

It is important to remember that Engels was a theorist and author in his own right. However much he willingly played second fiddle to Marx, he was no mere promoter or assistant. Engels collaboration with Marx involved independent intellectual activity. It may be said that Engels gave Marx not only the necessary funding but also vital intellectual contributions. Though these two were very different in many ways somehow they complemented each other.

Expulsion from Paris

Of course, Marx's consistent hostility to anything that suggested a restoration of the old feudal medieval order continued to get him in hot water. In January 1845, King Louis Philippe of France received a protest from Alexander von

Humboldt, envoy of the Prussian king. The protest concerned the insults flowing from the pages of left-wing *Vorwarts!* The end result was the newspaper's suspension two weeks later. Consequently, the French interior minister Francois Guizot ordered Karl Marx to leave France. With the rest of continental Europe closed to him, Marx was forced to pledge good conduct to King Leopold I in order to gain residency in Belgium. Although secure for the moment in Brussels with a 1,500 franc advance from a publisher and another 1,000 francs collected by Engels, the latter warned that in the end "you'll be left with no alternative but England." Meanwhile Jenny Marx, who was pregnant again, was forced to abandon the cultural heights of Paris for boring, dull Brussels.

Marx, soon to be followed by his wife and their nine-month-old daughter, arrived in Belgium in early February 1845. The police forbade Marx from publishing anything on contemporary politics, and thus reduced his possibilities for supporting himself and his family. Karl Marx was no better maintaining capital than making it. He soon went through his publisher's advance as well as other funds collected. Engels saved the situation when he donated all his first royalties of *The Condition of the Working Class in England* to the Marx family. However, other problems persisted as the Prussian government immediately began to pressure the Belgians to expel Marx from their territory. By the end of 1845, Marx felt compelled to renounce his Prussian citizenship, in the hope of losing his "privilege" of being hounded out of country after country by "his" government. Engels joined Marx in King Leopold's kingdom in April 1845.

During this same period, one of the von Westphalen family servants, Hellene Demuth, known as Lenchen to the Marx family, came to help young Jenny with the house work. She was to remain part of the family from then on. It was her practical nature, thriftiness, prudent decisiveness, and her selflessness that helped the Marx family come through crisis after crisis, as well as a host of day-to-day chores that often overtaxed the Marxes. They were all on solid theoretical ground when they discussed changing society, but often a bit out of their league when it came to changing bed clothes.

The German Ideology

During the winter of 1845–1846, Marx and Engels threw themselves into a work that was completed within six months. They gave it the title *The German Ideology* and shopped around for a publisher willing to print their manuscript. Finding no takers, Marx later said they had to leave the manuscript to "the nibbling criticism of the mice." In fact, *The German Ideology* would not appear until issued by the Marx–Engels–Lenin Institute of the Soviet Union in 1932. *The German Ideology* most certainly was a failure as a publishing project. Still, the writing of it had helped Marx and Engels achieve an understanding of their previous views as they jointly struggled to fashion new theories.

In common with most contemporary dissidents, the two German radicals rejected the old order that relied on feudal tradition, princes, kings, and an unquestionable religious dogma. They welcomed the fresh breeze of capitalist development with the attendant industrialization that would sweep away the "dead weight of tradition." Where Marx and Engels were unique was that they saw the downside of industrial capitalist development. The baron replaced by the bourgeois, the oppressed serf liberated only to become a poverty-stricken wage worker, the straightjacket of religion supplanted by ruthless individualism. Marx and Engels would praise industrial capitalism yet still find it wanting in its treatment of the common people. As Europe moved toward 1848 and revolution, this subtlety would elude most of their contemporaries. Even today, many find it hard to see industrialization as positive all the while criticizing the negative effects on people and the ecology.

Communist Correspondence Committee

As Marx still labored on *The German Ideology* with Engels, the two joined other exiles in Brussels to found the Communist Correspondence Society in February 1846. Marx hoped to establish ties between French, English, and German socialists that would allow an exchange of information on the progress of the movement and organizing developments. "This is the step that the social movement must take in its *literary* work," Marx reasoned, "in order to overcome *national* narrowness." With the effort of Marx and his friends, correspondence committees became established shortly thereafter in London, Paris, Le Havre, Copenhagen, Cologne, Elberfeld, Hamburg, Kiel, Leipzig, and elsewhere throughout Europe.

The work went less than smoothly. On the one hand, there were the utopian communist ideas being promoted by the tailor Wilhelm Weitling. Despite Marx's best efforts to reason with Weitling, the latter clung to the rather optimistic view that communist revolution was about to take place in Germany at any moment. There were also the so-called "true" socialists who tried to replace the class struggle with a love of the people and a plan to reconcile oppressors and the oppressed. These people would, Marx feared, turn communism into a religion. In June 1846, Marx heard that the London communists were breaking with Weitling and his utopian ideas. The League of the Just was a collection of radicals who Marx had hoped to influence; that same year the League, or at least their most important members, became convinced of the general correctness of the theories of Marx and Engels. Both men joined the League, and during the summer of 1847 its London-based central committee changed the organizational name to the Communist League. November witnessed a congress held in London where Marx and Engels agreed to pen a pamphlet explaining the new organization. The Communist League was not a political party in any meaningful sense of that term, nor was it even a very important group, having at most five hundred members. In fact, the main contribution it made to history was asking two relatively unknown German radicals to write a manifesto.

A Specter Is Haunting Europe?

Introduction

Widely known but little understood, the *Manifesto of the Communist Party*, or simply the *Communist Manifesto*, remains the most widely read work by Marx and Engels. It was not meant to be more than a popular, easy-to-read summation of their ideas. Neither author thought it had any immediate world-shaking importance, as the first edition in February 1848 consisted of only one thousand copies. Moreover, they both realized it for what it was, namely the product of a certain time and place in history. As times changed, the *Manifesto* would be lacking in this or that detail. As early as 1852, Engels wrote that Australia and California, not seriously considered in 1848, were both examples of developments not accounted for in the *Manifesto*. All the same, by 1918, the *Manifesto* had been published in thirty-five different languages and appeared in 544 separate editions.

Writing what was to become a classic of political theory did not come easily. The first draft was completed by Engels around June 1847 and took the form of a series of questions and answers. "1. What is Communism? Communism is the doctrine of the conditions of the liberation of the proletariat." In this format, the work followed the tradition of underground organizations with their confessions of faith, secret rites, and rituals. Engels and Marx concluded that this form was not the best way of presenting their ideas and moved on. However, they did not move quickly.

Although they had been charged to produce the manifesto as soon as possible, Marx seemed in no great hurry. In mid-December 1847, he gave a series of lectures on political economy for the German Workers' Association in Brussels, wrote articles for the radical press, and generally found excuses to postpone the work promised the Communist League. Toward the end of January 1848, the Central Committee in London was reaching the end of their patience. They issued an ultimatum to Marx demanding the manifesto by the first day of February. With the pressure of a deadline hanging over his head, Marx hurriedly took a pen in hand and frantically threw together the *Communist Manifesto*. Although he drew heavily on the Engels draft, later published as *The Principles of Communism*, the writing is pure Marx and a lot like poetry. For example, where a typical academic would have written "The European elites are concerned about social unrest," Marx writes, "A specter [ghost] is haunting Europe—the specter of communism."

Communism and Socialism before Marx and Engels

Actually the ghost of communism had haunted Europe long before the births of Marx or Engels. As Marx was quick to admit, communism and socialism—the two terms are often used to mean the same thing—were far from being an invention of the authors of the *Communist Manifesto*. These doctrines had been around for ages. Some have supporting evidence as far back as ancient Greece and Rome. Engels argued in a famous essay published near the end of his life that socialism was the basis for early Christianity. Noting the "points of resemblance" between early Christians and modern socialists, Engels stated both were movements of oppressed people which preached "forthcoming salvation from bondage and misery" and were "persecuted and baited" by the authorities.

Sir (Catholic saint) Thomas More's novel *Utopia*, penned during the reign of Henry VIII, is often called the first English socialist work. During the Reformation in Central Europe, the Reverend Thomas Muntzer preached against the wealthy and powerful as the spiritual leader of the German Peasant Revolt of 1525. What he and his followers wanted is typically considered a Christian communist community. In the social turmoil that accompanied the English Civil War of the 1640s, a group of common people emerged who were known as the "levelers" because of their democratic demands. This same period in England saw a small group of Christian communists, called the "diggers," who attempted to set up agricultural settlements, only to have them destroyed by the

Map 2.1 Revolutions of 1848

landowners. In these communities, all would share both the work and the rewards with the land being held in common. The following century, during the French Revolution of 1789, there was a man named Babeuf who organized an unsuccessful "Conspiracy of Equals."

More immediately before Marx's time, there was what he and Engels called the "utopian socialists," including Comte de Saint-Simon, Francois-Charles Fourier, and Robert Owen. Popular in the period between the Napoleonic Wars and the Revolutions of 1848, these thinkers commonly stressed that preexisting theories and ideas prevented the realization of human harmony and happiness. Having come to adulthood in a world with little or no industry, the utopians believed they could transform the world by demonstrating their superior ideas, preferably through individual examples. This contrasts with Marx, who emphasized the *class* nature of the existing state and societal institutions. He believed that conflict between social classes and political struggles would change society, not noble examples or theories.

Still, for all their criticism, Marx and Engels credited these individuals with laying the basis for modern socialism. Their ideas, although fuzzy or imprecise, helped to popularize socialism and certain key concepts. Saint-Simon, for example, saw an antagonism between those who labored and those who were idle. For him, those who labored included not only workers but also merchants, bankers, and manufacturers. All the problems plaguing society could be solved by applying the idea that "all men ought to work." Seeing the French Revolution as a struggle between those who worked and those who did not, Saint-Simon understood, only "in embryo" according to Marx and Engels, the role of economic conditions as the basis of history.

Likewise, Marx and Engels considered Fourier a contributor to the development of socialism. Engels notes approvingly, "He was the first to declare in any given society, the degree of woman's emancipation is the natural measure of the general emancipation." They further credited Fourier with producing an interesting analysis of history, whereby the past was divided into the stages of savagery, barbarism, patriarchate, and civilization.

While Saint-Simon and Fourier were in many ways products of the 1789 Revolution in France, early industrialization in Great Britain formed the context of Robert Owen's life. The reforms he instituted at his New Lanark cotton mills in Scotland electrified Europe. Owen reduced working hours, raised wages, and provided education for his workers, yet still amassed large profits. For most reformers, this notable accomplishment would have been enough, but not for Owen, who came to see that his workers "were slaves at my mercy." Not slaves in the classical, legal sense but slaves in as much as they needed the work Owen gave them to survive. Appalled by this realization, Owen, therefore, resolved to establish communistic industrial colonies where all would share in the profits of industrialization. These utopian experiments, including one established in New Harmony, Indiana, were failures, but Owen was unbowed. He spent the rest of his life, and a considerable fortune, fighting for labor reform. Among his greatest successes was the 1819 parliamentary bill, which limited the working hours of women and children in British factories.

The utopians sought to change society by the power of their ideas or by the power of examples. To the authors of the *Manifesto*, these men did not understand that those with power and wealth would never relinquish their positions of their own free will—individual exceptions like Owen not withstanding. The barons of wealth and privilege, like the feudal lords before them, could only be moved by force, and for Marx that force would be wielded by the democratically organized might of the working class. Presenting a prototype of a new and better society would never be enough. Change would have to be achieved by those who had "nothing to lose but their chains."

The socialism of earlier eras, no matter how noble, suffered from a fatal flaw. Its ideas were brought forth in times when the pre-industrial conditions precluded their success. Only with the dramatically expanded productivity afforded by the Industrial Revolution would it actually be possible to have an egalitarian society. Even if the communists and socialists of earlier times had triumphed, all they would have been able to offer was an equality of want. Before industrialization, there was no way to provide all people with decent housing, food, education, and material goods.

What Marx did was to take socialist moral beliefs and tie them to a theory of historical development. Many previous socialist theories essentially proposed a new type of morality. Like the early Christians, they advocated a more just distribution of goods based on a new morality. Marx made socialism a theory of production more than distribution. He also stressed political conflict/class conflict as opposed to moral witnessing or avocation. Marx thought that social change would ultimately require force. Not individual terrorism such as the anarchists, but force all the same. He hoped that the change would be largely peaceful but doubted that the old status quo would give up power without a fight. He pointed to the example of the American Civil War to illustrate the change he was making in socialism. For decades, well-meaning people had tried to convince slave owners of the immorality of the slave system with little result. Slavery was only ended when the slave owners revolted and their revolt was suppressed by force.

Industrial Capitalism: Pros and Cons

One striking thing about Marx writing in his *Manifesto* is that he spends so much time praising capitalists, or the bourgeoisie as he likes to call them, and their Industrial Revolution. Whereas many social critics only lamented the various negative effects of industrialization, Marx noted the positive effects as well. While mindful of all the human suffering that the Industrial Revolution had unleashed, Marx all the same credited it with freeing people from the stagnation and oppression of the old feudal ways.

The *Herr Doktor* from Trier may have wished for an end to capitalism, but he certainly took time to celebrate that very same capitalism's victory over ancient medieval society. When he said the "bourgeoisie, historically, has played a most revolutionary part," he meant it. While lauding the capitalist challenge to medieval superstition and hierarchy, Marx pointed out that the bourgeoisie only replaced exploitation "veiled by religious and political illusions" with "naked, shameless, direct, brutal exploitation." So, if he found a fault with capitalism, it was because it too failed to completely free people. Still, compared with feudalism, with its hereditary aristocracy, capitalism and the bourgeoisie win every time in Marx's book. As a leading London-based business journal noted on February 14, 2009, "Marx thought 'the bourgeoisie has played a most revolutionary part' in history. And although *The Economist* rarely sees eye to eye with the father of communism, on this Marx was right."

Marx praises the Industrial Revolution. In the *Communist Manifesto*, we read how the bourgeoisie have

> been the first to show what man's activity can bring about. It has accomplished wonders far surpassing Egyptian pyramids, Roman aqueducts and Gothic cathedrals; it has conducted expeditions that put in the shade all former exoduses of nations and crusades. The bourgeoisie cannot exist without con-

stantly revolutionizing the instruments of production, and thereby the relations of production, and with them the whole relations of society.

In other words, industrialization and the bourgeoisie were extremely positive in Marx's view. But his love affair with industrial progress in no way blinded him to the downside of this new world.

The industrial bourgeoisie has created "enormous cities" and "has thus rescued a considerable part of the population from the isolation of rural life," say Marx and Engels. On the downside, there is the "epidemic of overproduction" and depressions. "Society finds itself put back into state of momentary barbarism; it appears as if a famine, a universal war of devastation, had cut off the supply of every means of subsistence; industry and commerce seem to be destroyed."

On one side, the Industrial Revolution gave birth to massive levels of productive ability and commodities too numerous to be imagined in previous times, yet it also creates new developments like "the extensive use of machinery and to the division of labor [cause the worker to become] an appendage of the machine." These have profound social consequences as humans serve machines rather than vice versa. Nor is the Industrial Revolution worse only for craftsmen and unskilled laborers; in the *Communist Manifesto*, Marx argues that small business, shopkeepers, and farmers gradually sink into the working class because they do not have enough capital to compete on the vast scale of modern industry. Even in the twenty-first century, corporations such as WalMart and Microsoft are still attempting to eliminate their competition. For Marx, all who worked for others, all who were forced to sell their labor-power to the capitalists, were workers. Whether they were engaged in heavy physical labor or nicely dressed in an accounting office adding up long columns of numbers or today working on computers, if you worked for someone else you were most likely a worker. Now, workers may not think of themselves as a proletarian. Rather, they may think of themselves as a free individual. Marx realized this but still thought that "The advance of industry, whose involuntary promoter is the bourgeoisie, replaces the isolation of the laborers, due to competition, by their revolutionary combination, due to association. The development of modern industry, therefore, cuts from under its feet the very foundation on which the bourgeoisie produces and appropriates products."

Globalization

One prediction of the *Communist Manifesto* widely ridiculed at the time of its 1848 publication was that of a global market surpassing national industry and commerce. After all, in 1848, there were relatively few indications of what we today call "globalization." That did not stop Marx from arguing that industrialization "has drawn from under the feet of industry the national ground on which it stood. All old-established national industries have been destroyed or are daily being destroyed. They are dislodged by new industries, whose introduction becomes a life and death question for all civilized nations, by industries whose products are consumed, not only at home, but in every quarter of the globe." He even went on to say, "In place of old wants, satisfied by the productions of the country, we find new wants, requiring for their satisfaction the products of distant lands and climes. In place of the old local and national seclusion and self-sufficiency, we have intercourse in every direction, universal interdependence of nations." Today, in the twenty-first century, this no longer sounds so irrational.

If all of this seems to suggest that Marx was fraught with ambivalence about industrialism, it is because he was. In the one moment, he saw in it a potentially liberating force greater than any in recorded history, freeing humanity from ignorance, poverty, and superstition. Yet, true to Hegel's dialectic, Marx feared that human emancipation would be pushed off to a remote future as those who owned the means of production busied themselves with their own enrichment rather than society's progress. If only those pulled into the industrial process as proletarians could gain political power, then Marx felt that the wonder of this new world might be thrown open to all. Further, Marx could be practical, and some would even say cynical—as well as visionary. He noted that the bourgeoisie would even hold back technological advancement if it threatened their profits. Following this logic, one late twentieth-century social critic, Ralph Nader, argued the only reason the world had yet to convert to solar power was that the oil companies could not patent the sun. Similarly, Marx feared that the captains of industry would overlook human need if it interfered with share-value enhancement. Therefore, his thinking was somewhat paradoxical. He was the biggest booster of industrial capitalism while remaining its fiercest critic.

Revolutionary Storms

As the first copies of the *Communist Manifesto* trickled from the printing press, Paris broke out in revolution. The liberal French king Louis Philippe, also known as Louis the Pear because of his physical composition, abdicated after only a few days of street fighting in February 1848. Called the Banker King because of his closeness to the financial sector, Louis Philippe fled to London with little resistance. The insurgency spread beyond the French capital. On March 13, the workers of Vienna constructed barricades and Austrian chancellor Metternich, who reconstructed the conservative European order after the defeat of Napoleon Bonaparte, left office and ran for his life. In Prussia, that feudal bastion in northeastern Germany, the revolution began with an uprising of the Polish people living under Berlin's yoke. Fighting fiercely against the occupying Prussian forces, the Polish Uprising of 1848 shook Prussia's aristocracy. By March 18, the revolt had even spread to Berlin, capital of reactionary Prussia. After a night of deadly street fighting between workers and the king's troops, soldiers began to disobey their officers' orders. This made it necessary for the king to give in to the crowds and withdraw his troops from Berlin on March 19. Fearing for his throne, if not his life, the King of Prussia promised to introduce liberal reforms and meld Prussia into a united Germany. It seemed that the revolution had succeeded, but Marx quickly realized that this was an illusion.

In 1848, Germany was a geographic area with a common culture and language rather than a nation-state. That is, "Germany" was a collection of more than three dozen countries—some were large like Prussia while most were little more than city-states. For some time, there had been increasingly strong sentiment for unifying Germany, much like there was one united France. Of course, it was not that simple, since even those who wanted a united Germany were divided on whether to include German-speaking Austria with her vast non-Germanic Empire.

There was also the question of what form of government this hypothetical nation should have: republic or monarchy. Marx, not surprisingly, was a firm supporter of the idea of the republican form of government. However, Germany would not come into existence until 1871, and then only as a semi-constitutional monarchy centered in Prussian Berlin.

Early in 1848, the issue was yet to be settled. Liberal pressure, particularly from businessmen, caused a number of hereditary rulers to abdicate or resign from their thrones. In many places, mass protests and meetings demanded freedom of the press and assembly, a national German parliament, and even arming of the common people. At this time, nationalism was associated with liberalism and republicanism, whereas the old landed aristocracy appeared more interested in its dynasty than the nation. The economic situation of the average German deteriorated as poor harvests in 1846 and 1847 led to widespread hunger, and conditions for those who fled to work in the cities were terrible. In the urban areas, workers faced long working hours, virtual starvation wages, and almost no legal rights. So while the liberal republicans fought for free trade against existing feudal restrictions, the average worker and peasant were far more concerned with equality and social security over capitalist economic freedom.

As Marx feared, the leadership of the revolutionary movement fell to the better-educated—and less militant—liberals. Their great accomplishment was the Frankfurt Parliament, which was to create a new German government for a new nation-state. In reality, the parliament debated endlessly but did little. Engels went so far as to lampoon the Frankfurt politicians for being the unfortunate victims of a new disease, "parliamentary cretinism." This "disease" caused the unfortunate victim to lose all touch with reality and labor under the delusion that all world events turned on the speeches given, and votes taken, in the legislative body favored by the victim's presence. Neither Marx nor Engels contracted this "disease."

Both knew that what was needed in order to depose the old crowned heads was military force. Unlike Oliver Cromwell and the forces of parliament in the English Revolution of the seventeenth century, the Frankfurt Assembly made no serious attempt at organizing a military. Further, there was a lack of organized political parties and strong leadership, both of which contributed to the success of the 1789 French Revolution. With many scattered proposals but no broad agreement, the assembly agonized endlessly over exactly what should, or should not, be incorporated into the new Germany. There was also great tension between Catholics and Protestants, neither of whom wanted to be in a new Germany if it was dominated by their religious rivals. At one point, the representatives gathered in Frankfurt went so far as to offer the reactionary Prussian king Fredrick Wilhelm IV a chance to become king of all Germany. He turned them down reportedly saying he "would not accept a crown from the gutter."

Marx and Engels during the 1848 Revolution

After receiving the first news from Berlin, Marx was convinced that illusions were widely held between the working class and "petty bourgeoisie," the lower middle class. Both groups thought that the apparent elevation of a number of big businessmen into the political system would result in profound changes. Marx felt it his duty to warn them of the profound disillusionment that was likely to follow. By the end of March, Marx and Engels drafted a program under the impressive-sounding title *Demands of the Communist Party in Germany*. The title is rather misleading because they really had nothing like a party, Communist or otherwise. What Marx had were scattered groupings that had, more or less, sympathy for his views but acted completely independently.

On April 11, 1848, Marx and Engels went to Cologne, where the former had once worked as editor of the *Rheinische Zeitung*. For a short time, Marx hoped that the Communist League might provide some sort of direction to the spontaneously developing radical movement. This optimism was short-lived as letters from friends throughout Germany soon convinced Marx that the couple hundred League members were but a drop in the churning sea of revolt. Marx now faced a difficult dilemma: He and his comrades could stay out of the movement and instead calmly analyze events. Fearing that such a turn to sectarianism would isolate him and his friends, Marx decided to join the existing democratic movement in the hope of gaining an audience with the populace. Along with Engels, he concluded that a united front against the old feudal order was more important than their distrust of business-dominated organizations. Not everyone agreed with this approach, which was shown by the decision of the Cologne Workers' Association to boycott the May elections called by the Frankfurt Assembly. Although Marx agreed that the indirect voting system set up was undemocratic and designed to limit working people's influence, he still felt that radicals should participate in elections. Finally, Marx recognized that his time was best spent making use of the newly won freedom of the press.

He would establish a newspaper as a vehicle for his political ideas—the *Neue Rheinische Zeitung* with the subtitle *An Organ of Democracy*. Setting up a new publication is no easy business in the best of times. In this regard, 1848 was certainly not the best of times. First, there was a shortage of the necessary funds. Many people who may have supported the idea had little or no money. Wealthy liberals may have had the surplus cash, but they were doubtful about advancing it to a person of Marx's political beliefs. Even Engels, with his connections to the industrial world, came up short. On April 25, he reported his failures, including an attempt to get money from his father who would "rather spray us with a thousand canisters of grapeshot." Marx determined that the working capital for the paper should be 30,000 thalers; a thaler being a currency unit then used in Germany. Attempts were made to raise the funds by selling shares at fifty thalers apiece, but by May only 13,000 thalers had been collected.

All the same, on May 31, the first issue of the *Neue Rheinische Zeitung-An Organ of Democracy* appeared in Cologne. While the paper was a cooperative effort, there was no doubt as to the prime mover: the thirty-year-old Karl Marx. The paper fought openly for the replacement of Prussian and Austrian despotism by a united and democratic republic. Marx ruthlessly attacked the Frankfurt Assembly as indecisive, with only a minority of true democrats. It was this wavering and compromising attitude on the part of Germany's would-be parliament that encouraged a counterrevolution by the feudal lords. The articles in the first issue were sharply written—so much so that the *Neue Rheinische Zeitung* lost half of its stockholders. Within two weeks of the first issue hitting the street, the storm Marx had predicted hit Berlin. On June 14, Berlin workers attacked the arsenal and seized weapons that the king and his big bourgeois allies refused to give them. Poorly organized, the revolt was quickly put down. Marx thundered that the Prussian bourgeoisie had betrayed democracy by allying with the monarchy. Only if the common people could have a say in government could a truly democratic and united Germany be established.

Marx and his supporters also protested against the betrayal of the peasants. In the first weeks of the revolution, the peasants had, by themselves, eliminated feudal service and duties imposed by their "lords." Instead of passing legislation to support this new reality, as the French bourgeoisie had done in 1789, the Prussian leaders of business chose to support the status quo and return the peasantry to their oppressed state. Another concern for both Marx and Engels was the situation of oppressed national minorities like the Poles. In their press, they argued that a nation cannot be free itself if it denies freedom to other nations. When, in the spring of 1848, Poles demanded independence from Prussia, the government answered them with superior firepower and massacres of civilians. If Prussia was the backbone of reaction in Germany, it was backed up by tsarist Russia, the protector of feudalism throughout Europe.

As the *Neue Rheinische Zeitung* attacked the liberal big bourgeoisie for their betrayals, it saw small business as real allies for the workers and peasants. After all, these three social classes all had the same common interest in the establishment of democracy and a republican Germany. In spite of the never-ending shortage of money, the *Neue Rheinische Zeitung* reached a circulation of 5,000 copies in less than four months. At this moment in time, there were not that many newspapers with larger circulations. Meanwhile, many other democratic and workers' papers in Germany and elsewhere began to reprint its articles.

Events from France soon shaped the entire European situation. On June 23, 1848, the workers of Paris rose up in defense of their own class interests. After days where much blood was shed, on June 26, the workers were defeated. Thousands of proletarians were brutally murdered by the French government's soldiers. To their injury came insult from the established press throughout Europe, calling the Paris workers social scum, thieves, and worse. Marx saw them instead as heroes, saying "to place the laurel wreath on their darkened heads that is the privilege that is the duty of the democratic press." This solidarity with the defeated Parisian workers cost Marx most of his remaining shareholders. What is more important, with the defeat in Paris, reactionary forces in Germany knew it was time to launch their own offensive.

The Empires Strike Back

In July 1848, Marx was ordered to appear before the Cologne court, charged with insulting the police and the civilian authorities, as the offices of the *Neue Rheinische Zeitung* were searched. The cause for this was that the paper had reported on the police raid against the Cologne Workers' Association, as well as the arrest of two of its leaders. The paper reported that the raid occurred with great brutality, including the rough manhandling of a pregnant woman. Although not a member of the Workers' Association, Marx, a member of the separate Democratic Society, felt that all the forces on the left had to unite against the ever-increasing attempt to return Germany to a prerevolutionary situation. These parties were far from permanent institutions having both changing ideas and shifting memberships. So it comes as no surprise that things were not to be as successful as Marx would have liked, due to personality conflicts and the usual sectarian infighting.

All the same, the representatives of the old order were becoming increasingly disturbed by the popularity of the *Neue Rheinische Zeitung*. Existing laws made banning the publication difficult, and such blatant suppression of free speech would cause a radical response from the common people. So instead they refused to recognize the chief editor, Marx, as a Prussian subject, and thus he could be expelled at anytime as a "foreigner." Perhaps in response, Marx began to travel to Berlin, Vienna, and back to Berlin again. Everywhere he spoke, Marx emphasized the need for a common front against the feudal lords and their big-bourgeois allies. He likewise pleaded for funds to continue publication of the *Neue Rheinische Zeitung*. Whereas most Germans kept their wallets closed, a meeting of Polish democrats turned more than 2,000 thalers to him for continued publication.

Returning to Cologne on September 12, Marx found the political situation turning rapidly against democracy and the movement. A crisis had developed in Prussia between the elected assembly and the monarchy. An attempt to purge the army of counterrevolutionary officers, and making the forces pledge allegiance to the constitution, failed. The king felt confident enough to impose a new reactionary government. Berlin was recaptured by King Wilhelm's troops, and his order was restored. In November, the monarchy, now safely reestablished, dissolved the Prussian parliament and issued his own constitution. This document, while making a few nominal concessions to the winds of democracy that shook his throne, kept ultimate authority with the king and created a parliament that was class-based, so as 80 percent of the population would elect only a third of the seats in the lower house. The rest would be chosen by their "better" elements of society.

In place after place throughout Central Europe, revolutionaries who fought for democracy or more freedom were attacked and ultimately fell even if resistance lingered well into 1849. In Austria, Imperial Hapsburg troops launched an offensive against Vienna on October 23. The revolution there was drowned in blood after over a week of brave but hopeless resistance from workers and students. An all-German workers' association was founded in Leipzig in June 1849. The flame of revolution even flared up on occasion as Dresden workers stormed the arsenal and demanded the Saxon king to recognize the proposed liberal constitution. Prussian troops were quickly called in and the rebels were able to hold out for only six days. As the last rebels fled Dresden, fighting broke out in the Rhineland, Westphalia, in Baden, and in the Palatinate. Still, these were to be the death agony rather than the birth pains, of the democratic revolution.

By spring 1849, the future of Marx's *Neue Rheinische Zeitung* was grim. Marx had an expulsion order issued against him on May 11 and Engels could expect arrest at any time. The *Neue Rheinische Zeitung* stood accused of "subversion against the government, its violent overthrow and the creation of a social republic." Marx attempted to hand off editorial control to save the paper, only to have the government proclaim it would banish any editor. Realizing the hopelessness of continuing publication in the context of the increasing repression, Marx edited a final issue on May 19. The final issue of the *Neue Rheinische Zeitung* was printed completely in red ink. The farewell thanked their readers for their support, warned against irresponsible armed adventures, and noted that their last words would be always and everywhere "emancipation of the working class."

By selling off everything, including the printing press and the furniture from his house, Marx was able to pay off the debts of the *Neue Rheinische Zeitung*, but he was left penniless, and the family silver went to the pawnshop. After his family left to stay with his mother-in-law in Trier, Marx joined Engels in a journey to Frankfurt, where they attempted to persuade the assembled delegates to support the insurgents in southwestern Germany. Failing at this, they proposed unsuccessfully to have the revolutionary troops march on Frankfurt. However, they did have a friendly meeting with an old comrade, Willich, and Engels promptly volunteered to join the revolutionary corps. Neither Marx's health nor his personality suited military service, so he journeyed to Paris. There, he would witness the revolution that had begun in Paris, and watched it die in Paris as government troops crushed protests and arrested radical leaders. Expelled from Paris, and with Germany and Belgium closed to him, Karl Marx sailed into Dover in England on August 27, 1849, on board the *SS City of Boulogne*. Heading right to London, Marx immediately wrote Engels, who was in Switzerland, to join him there in an exile that would last the rest of their lives.

London: Into Exile and Poverty

Introduction

London, by the middle of the nineteenth century, was a massive place with several million residents. It was called by many the workshop of the world, and it was thought by some to be the greatest city on the planet. It was undeniably the heart of the Industrial Revolution that was just starting to sweep the Western world. Great Britain itself was changing, as the 1851 census revealed that the majority of the population, for the first time in history, was living in towns. When Marx reached London in late August 1849, he was only one of the hundreds of political refugees drawn by the English capital's reputation for taking in those whom the authorities of continental Europe spit out. A great portion of the most active members of the Communist League journeyed to London around the same time, and for the same reasons, as Karl Marx.

The London that gave the tired revolutionaries of Europe a place to flee was also a city that contained unspeakable slums. Infectious disease was widespread, including episodic cholera outbreaks, as the city's drinking water was contaminated by the filth emptied into its sewers. London's infamous fog was more a product of industry's unregulated air pollution than any natural occurrence. Large sections of the urban area were recognizable by their wretched smell. Purportedly, three thousand houses of prostitution operated at the time. To the German political refugees, these horrors only added to the shock of arriving in a strange country whose tongue and traditions were alien to them. With few exceptions these Germans came to London without money, and they found a city that honored wealth above all else.

Marx was not one of the exceptions. He was as penniless and unemployed as most of his less educated countrymen. When Jenny, the three children, and their helper Lenchen came in September, the situation became even graver as Mrs. Marx was in an advanced state of pregnancy. At first, even ever-loyal Engels was unable to help financially, as he too was without funds. In November 1849, the Marxes' second son, named Heinrich Guido, was born. Guido died suddenly about a year later causing tremendous grief to Karl and Jenny. Despite their own suffering, the Marx family did everything it could to help their fellow exiles. Given their own dire circumstances, the best they could do was raising a little money from slightly better-off political supporters. Still, their main work was to give moral support to emigrants struggling in the new land.

While Marx had precious little money, he was highly educated. He put his academic training to good use by giving lectures to refugees in subjects ranging from Greek to contemporary political economy. Being more than a bit of a show-off, he loved outwitting those among his students who thought they had found a weakness in his argument. All the same, all the accounts that survive indicate that Marx was also a dedicated if not inspiring educator. Among his students was a young German named Wilhelm Liebknecht, who later co-founded the German Social Democratic Party (SPD). Liebknecht always saw Marx as his mentor, even if in private Marx would often grow frustrated with his former pupil and denounce him as a "fool" in letters to Engels.

Poverty of the Early Years

For the better part of their first decade on English soil, the Marx family lived little better than the indigenous London poor, who were among the worst off in Europe. During their first winter in London, the whole family lived in one room, for which they had to pay a huge rent. When their funds ran out, the landlady moved to evict the Marxes. (In a letter to family friend Joseph Weydemeyer, Jenny Marx described the horror of the eviction: "Two bailiffs came into the house, requisitioned all my little possessions, beds, linens, clothing, everything, including the cradle of my poor child, the better toys of the girls, who watched with hot tears in their eyes." When the local baker, butcher, milkman, and other assorted merchants appeared to demand payment due, Jenny sold their remaining beds to pay off the debt.) None of this endeared the capitalist system to Herr Doktor Marx, his wife, or family.

Marx largely refrained from including his firsthand experiences or impressions of industrial society in his writings. This is unlike Engels who wrote *The Condition of the Working Class in England.* Nevertheless, Marx was doubtless molded by his poverty in London. It could not be otherwise for someone who argued that "being determines consciousness." For an individual who once aspired to the pleasant lifestyle afforded honored German professors, the poverty endured in London surely left its mark. One can only imagine how Marx felt when compelled to write family friend Weydemeyer on October 29, 1850, asking him to borrow money and redeem the Marx family silver "in the Frankfurt pawnshop, then sell the silver to a goldsmith or to anybody who buys such things there, pay the man from whom you borrowed, and send the remainder to me." "My situation is now such," Marx continued that, "I must under any circumstances raise some money in order to be able to continue working." So depending on gifts from comrades, above all Engels, and other meager sources of income the Marx household would find their possessions with the pawnbrokers or recently reclaimed.

Sometime during 1853, a Prussian police spy visited the Marx family in London leaving a very detailed account of their circumstances. The spy comments that Jenny Marx is "an educated, pleasant lady [who] feels quite at home in this misery." Meanwhile Marx is seen as leading a disorderly existence. "Washing, grooming and changing underwear," the spy concludes, "are rarities with him; he gets drunk readily." Marx was so addicted to smoking tobacco that on entering his room "one gropes as if in a cave until one gets gradually accustomed to the fumes and begins to distinguish objects as it in a fog."

Worse of all was the spy's description of the Marx family living quarters. They lived "in two rooms, the one with a view of the street is the living room; the one in the back is the bedroom. In the whole lodging not a single piece of good furniture is to be found; everything is broken, ragged and tattered; everything is covered with a finger-thick dust; everywhere the greatest disorder." In the living room stood a table where "lie manuscripts, books, newspapers, the children's' toys, the scraps of his wife's sewing, tea cups with broken rims, dirty spoons, knives and forks, candlesticks, inkwell, drinking glasses ... everything piled up helter-skelter."

Given such a bitter living situation, it is not surprising that it took a toll on Karl, Jenny, and the children. Despite having an intellectual understanding of the reasons behind his poverty, Marx often erupted in irrational rages. He ranted against various individuals, particularly creditors and money lenders, and the world in general. Some have even argued that he internalized some of his rage and that this accounts for his frequent bouts of illness. Jenny suffered from a nervous condition and became convinced that at least three of her children died because of the poverty that they lived in. When in 1855, Marx's surviving son Edgar became ill, things seem to be headed downward. Seven years old and the favorite of not just his father but the whole household, Edgar, nicknamed

"Colonel Musch," died in April 1855. He was the third Marx child to die and the family was devastated.

Another death helped to save the Marx family from its intolerable situation. They were able to move to a much better place with two floors, a garden, and seven rooms in 1856 when Jenny inherited money upon the death of her mother Baroness von Westphalen. Perhaps self-consciously, Jenny Marx noted that this move was part of the family's march toward "becoming bourgeois." Despite all this personal turmoil, Marx remained wedded to the idea of human progress. In the Industrial Revolution, he saw the dawn of the replacement of a society based on the painful toil of the many, by a world where machines would produce material abundance for all. The exiled German thinker believed that industrialization could either liberate humanity into a world of ease and democracy, or alternatively, it could produce a form of oppression more insidious and all encompassing than ever before.

Into the British Museum

In London, Marx would also gain a certain detachment from the day-to-day chaos of politics so common on the continent of Europe. While he still spent much, some would say wasted, time in political infighting, exile afforded Karl Marx the chance to reflect on industrial capitalism as it unfolded before his eyes. Moreover, the British authorities saw little point in harassing political radicals as long as they appeared to pose no immediate threat to the public order. Thus situated as a free, if poor, resident of the English capital was determined to analyze the very industrialism that was all around him. This he did with a single-minded dedication that escapes most writers.

In many strange ways, exile for Karl Marx proved to be what a research sabbatical is for a modern academic, which is a time to distance one from day-to-day distractions and to concentrate on a certain project. Removed from the ferment of continental Europe, Marx had the time and the distance to reflect upon what the changes in the economy really signified. He was well placed for his research, as he had access to the collections of the British Museum. Whatever his predilections or prejudices, Karl Marx considered himself a person of science. Therefore it was vital for his writings, particularly those on economics, to be based on what he saw as solid, generally agreed-upon evidence. Marx was quick to accept many of the basics of British political economy. It was more the use the theories were put to that troubled him. Day after day, in fair weather and foul, Karl Marx dragged himself to the British Museum searching for data. For enlightenment, he went to the British Museum.

An incident from Engels illustrates their understanding that they must avoid falling into rigidity in their view of science. The younger Engels had been convinced that nature followed a clear, rational evolution. When he first heard of a platypus, he assumed it was a hoax because it did not fit within his established theory of nature. After all, the platypus made no sense in Engels understanding of natural history. Later to his great embarrassment, he saw a living platypus in an English zoo. Thus, he, and Marx, learned the dangers of confusing science with an inflexible devotion to any established theory.

With origins in the eighteenth century, the British Museum was different from other research centers, in that its collections belonged to the nation, and admission was free to everyone. From the start, there was a reading room where scholars could consult the collections. In the nineteenth century, when earlier restrictions on access were abolished, not only Karl Marx, but also the British novelist Charles Dickens and the Russian revolutionary Vladimir Lenin, would take advantage of the British Museum Reading Room. When in June 1852, Karl Marx got his admission card to the reading room; it launched a period of intense study which saw Marx work almost daily from ten in the morning until seven in the evening. Filling notebook after notebook, Marx compiled data about the abuses of the industrial system while deepening his understanding of classical British political economy.

Louis Napoleon and Bonapartism

By overthrowing an elected government through force and deception, the seizure of power by Napoleon Bonaparte's nephew in France on December 12, 1851, provided Karl Marx with a political target worthy of his wit. Written within four months of Louis Napoleon's *coup d'etat*, *The Eighteenth Brumaire of Louis Bonaparte* reveals Marx at his best when analyzing specific historical events. Contrasting Bonaparte "the lesser" with his famous uncle Napoleon, Marx notes that history repeats itself, "the first time as tragedy, the second time as farce." Much more than a work of political invective, *The Eighteenth Brumaire* is an important work of materialist history and political theory. For example, Marx used it to discuss in detail the role that individuals play in the making of human history. He asserts that "Men make their own history, but they do not make it just as they please; they do not make it under circumstances chosen by themselves, but under circumstances directly encountered, given and transmitted from the past." In other words, ideas don't drop from the heavens but rise out of specific historical and social situations. People are not "born to greatness," rather circumstances come together to allow them to become "great."

This work also has a very thoughtful analysis of Bonapartism, a movement many have seen as a forerunner to the fascist movements of the twentieth century. Marx developed the idea that Bonapartism occurs when a group of counter-revolutionaries seizes power, and then doles out reforms and favors to co-opt the common people. This phenomenon occurs when there is a type of stand-off between the traditional ruling classes and a revolutionary movement, neither having the strength to impose its will on the other. In this situational stalemate, force is used to seize power in a manner that maintains the traditional ruling class's role, but at the same time hides this rule from the common people. So, Louis Napoleon played the part of a popular hero while pursuing policies that, in the main, served the French bourgeois capitalist class.

Thus the purpose of *The Eighteenth Brumaire* was, according to Marx, to "demonstrate how the class struggle in France created circumstances and relationships that made it possible for a grotesque mediocrity to play a hero's part." This analysis has been utilized by later writers to explain the rise of fascist regimes like those of Mussolini and Hitler, as well as populist dictatorships like Peron in Argentine. In all cases, the Bonapartist government utilized nationalist ideals and militarism to obscure its defense of the traditional elite.

New York Daily Tribune

During the decade of the 1850s, Karl Marx was fortunate to become a correspondent for the *New York Daily Tribune*. The income from the articles he wrote for the American newspaper would be his only steady sources of income for the better part of a decade. When in August 1851 Marx received a letter from Charles Dana, second in command to Horace Greeley on the *Daily Tribune*, he welcomed the invitation for more than financial reasons. The *Daily Tribune* was in many ways the most important American newspaper of its time, with a readership of 200,000. The readers tended to be educated and serious, hungering for substance in their news reporting rather than sensation. Marx would not have to change either his style or politics in order to write for Dana. However, his knowledge of English wasn't quite up to the task so Engels wrote articles about Germany for an entire year. These were published in New York under Marx's name.

Marx only began to write contributions to the *Daily Tribune* himself in August 1852, and even then he wrote in German and had ever-loyal Engels translate them into English. By 1853, Marx felt confident enough to write his *Daily Tribune* articles in English. Throughout the 1850s, Marx improved his English and his words eventually went from being wooden to terse to eloquent. For sources, he used other newspapers, such as the *Times* of London and the continental European press. For a long period, Marx wrote two articles a week, which were dispatched by steamship on Tuesdays and Fridays.

The editors of the *Daily Tribune* did not always act in a manner that pleased Marx or Engels. They altered text without explanation, and nearly a quarter of the articles he sent were published as unsigned editorials with Marx receiving no credit and little payment. On December 14, 1853, Engels received a letter from his London-based comrade in which Marx noted, "… the *Tribune* is making a great splash with your articles, *poor* Dana, no doubt, being regarded as their author. At the same time they have appropriated 'Palmerston,' which means that, for eight weeks past, Marx-Engels have virtually constituted the *Editorial staff* of the *Tribune*." This was to be a constant complaint, as another letter to Engels on April 22, 1854, bemoaned the fact that of "late the *Tribune* has again been appropriating all of my articles as leaders, and putting my name to nothing but rubbish." By 1860, the New York paper had printed more than 320 essays written by Marx. The *New York Daily Tribune* would not pay for articles they asked Marx to write but then failed to print. Moreover, payments were irregular, and cashing checks or money orders from the United States often proved troublesome. For a time, two articles were generally accepted weekly for an income of about twenty dollars per week. In March 1857, the editors reduced Marx's contribution to one essay a week, and thus in one blow cut his income in half. Marx's letters to Engels clearly indicated how worried he was by this pay cut since everything of value was already at the pawnshop. Soon even this work dried up, as the American public and the *Daily Tribune* became absorbed by the U.S. Civil War.

By 1862, the Marx family was deeply in debt, assignments from the *Daily Tribune* became rare, and an attempt to achieve a steady income as the London correspondent for the Viennese paper *Die Presse* came to little. With dark gallows humor, Marx wrote to Engels, "If only I knew how to start some *business*! Gray, dear friend, is all theory, and only *business* is green." [Emphasis in original] Engels was able to send about $25 a month to help out, but this was far from enough to keep the Marx family out of poverty.

The Crimean War

If life was peaceful in London, by 1853, the same could not be said for Western Asia. Napoleon the lesser, as Marx called the ruler of France, forced the weak Ottoman Empire to grant his nation "sovereign authority" in the Holy Land. This enraged the Tsar of the Russian Empire, who saw himself as the natural protector of people who were overwhelmingly Eastern Orthodox Christians living in the Middle East. With the failure of diplomacy, the Russians faced war not only with France but also with Great Britain, the Ottoman Empire, and the Kingdom of Sardinia. These often forgotten conflicts were to last three years and claim hundreds of thousands of lives, with as many as three-quarters of the fatalities being caused by disease.

Not surprisingly, this massive bloodbath attracted Marx's attention. He had long supported the struggles of Poles, Hungarians, and Italians for national independence while viewing the Tsar's Empire as the bulwark of everything reactionary and wrong in Europe. Thus, Marx supported the war against the Russian Empire as a struggle against the Tsar. He hoped that a defeat for the Russian army on the battlefield would be the signal for successful national liberation movements throughout the Tsar's far-flung possessions.

With mounting frustration, he watched as British Prime Minister Palmerston pursued the war with less than his nation's full energy. Despite the horrendous loss of life, Marx and Engels came to regard the Crimean conflict as a pseudo-war once it came to light that neither France nor England intended to launch any decisive campaign against the "Russian Bear." This hesitancy to strike a decisive blow against Tsarism piqued Marx's curiosity. Laborious research in the British Museum led Marx to read over stacks of official blue books and government records. He concluded that there had been secret cooperation between St. Petersburg and London since the time of Tsar Peter the Great. More shockingly, he decided that Prime Minister Palmerston was an instrument of Tsarist policy because of his supposed pro-Russian sentiments.

A more simple explanation was more likely, which is that Great Britain wanted to do nothing that would upset the balance of power in Europe. It would seem that Marx's hatred for the Tsar and his brutal empire may have caused him to misread the available evidence. In any case, his hostility to Lord Palmerston led him into contact with a very dubious Member of Parliament named David Urquhart. This Conservative M.P. had an almost pathological hatred of Russia combined with a passion for all things Turkish. In fact, he is widely credited with introducing the Turkish bath to England and once told Marx that one of his articles was so good "it could have been written by a Turk."

In all other matters, Urquhart was a conventional Conservative politician. Yet, after reading one of Marx's articles, Urquhart arranged a meeting. The two were united in their hatred for Palmerston but little else. Urquhart was deeply disappointed to find out that Marx was a revolutionary while the latter wrote Engels that the Conservative was a "monomaniac." Despite their profound political differences in most all things, the two managed for a time to cooperate in attacking the government of Lord Palmerston. Urquhart paid to print and distribute some of Marx's anti-Tsarist articles in editions from fifteen to thirty thousand. Given that they had nothing else in common, it is little wonder that their alliance was to be tentative and short-lived. Still, one may wonder if Marx was not wasting his time by working with a rank reactionary and a rather odd one at that. All in all, it was an experience that helped sharpen Marx's skills at political journalism and analysis.

British in India, Opium Wars in China

In spite of the financial uncertainties Marx experienced during his years with the *New York Daily Tribune*, the pages of the Greeley publication allowed Marx to present many of his radical ideas in a clear, reflective manner. It remains amazing to a twenty-first-century observer to read articles of such length, sophistication, and political slant while knowing that they actually appeared in a major, respectable American newspaper. In an essay entitled "The Future of British Rule in India" that appeared in the *Daily Tribune* on July 22, 1853, Marx began to outline his theory of imperialism. His moral condemnation of the colonial project was clear as he wrote of it that the "profound hypocrisy and inherent barbarism of bourgeois civilization lies unveiled before our eyes, turning from its home, where it assumes respectable forms, to the colonies, where it goes naked." Yet in the same article, he acknowledges how industrialism lays the foundation for a better world. The Industrial Revolution brings "the development of the productive powers of man and the transformation of material production into a scientific domination of natural agencies. Bourgeois industry and commerce create these material conditions of a new world in the same way as geological revolutions have created the surface of the earth."

As usual it was neither industry nor even globalization that Marx opposed. His criticisms were based in the *manner* that the rich countries treated their poor subjects at home and abroad. In other words, it was who *owned* the means of production that caused the misery, not the system of industrial production in and of itself. In one essay, he concluded that once "a great social revolution [seizes] the results of the bourgeois epoch, the market of the world and the modern powers of production, and subjected them to the common control of the most advanced peoples, then only will human progress cease to resemble that hideous, pagan idol, who would not drink the nectar but from the skulls of the slain." That is, democratic control would utilize the positive aspects of industrialism for development while minimizing the negatives of the system.

One also sees Marx's love–hate relation with international capitalism in his September 1858 article "Trade or Opium?" published in the *Daily Tribune*. He expressed his moral outrage at the British promotion of the opium trade and the human misery brought to China through the creation of countless addicts. He went so far as to quote approvingly an English critic who condemned the opium trade as being even more morally reprehensible than the slave trade. The argument was that in the latter the profiteers at least had to keep the Africans alive.

As he made the moral argument against the British-led opium trade, Marx shifted to his economic case. Citing the report of a committee from the British House of Commons, he pointed to the inability of the Chinese to purchase manufactured goods, since many used their silver, tea, and silk to pay for the imported opium. Marx contended that the expansion of Anglo-American industry would be one result of the suppression of the opium trade, insofar as China would have more capacity to absorb the products of industry. In other words, industrial expansion, by way of increased trade with China, clearly would be a positive good in this instance as it would develop the means of production in England and the United States and additionally eliminate the terrible social evil of drug addiction.

Marx's writings on colonialism are so often misunderstood because he saw both good and evil in forces of imperialism. To take India as an example, there he saw unsurpassed misery created by the British in their destruction of the native textile industry and neglect of public works. This was without a doubt the negative face of colonial intervention. On the positive side, Marx believed English industrialists had an interest in the advancement of the economy, particularly as shown by the creation of a railroad system. Moreover, Marx predicted that the requirements of modern industry would force British capital to create a new class of Indians, "endowed with the requirements for government, and imbued with European science." Not surprisingly, he believed that the Indians "will not reap the fruits of the new elements" until either the industrial working class seized control in Great Britain or the South Asian people "throw off the English yoke altogether." Once that happened, Marx fully expected the Asian people to use science to improve their societies.

The Irish Problem

One cannot speak of British colonialism in the nineteenth century without mentioning Ireland. Karl Marx, not to mention Engels, took a good deal of interest in Irish affairs, if for no other reason than that "Ireland has revenged herself upon English, socially—by bestowing an Irish quarter on every English industrial, maritime or commercial town of any size." This meant, of course, that the "Irish Question" could in no way be separated from the general condition of the common people in Great Britain. Further, the Irish and Ireland were always a major topic of discussion within English politics.

Marx wrote how the traditional "Irish agricultural system is being replaced by the English system, the system of small tenures by big tenures, and the modern capitalist is taking the place of the old landowner." This change was prepared by the "Potato Famine" of 1847 which left almost a million dead, and forced another million to flee their poverty and head to the United States, Canada, and Australia. The population of Ireland, which had been more than 8,000,000 in 1841, stood at only 5,850,309 by 1861. For the ten-year period of 1851–1861, the number of occupied houses fell by 52,990. This was more than the work of the famine, which Marx noted "killed the poor devils only." It was the capitalist revolution in agriculture that crushed Irish farmers, particularly the majority of the population who had less than hundred acres under cultivation. Forced by competition off the land, the displaced Irish farmer had few choices other than becoming a wage worker or leaving Ireland altogether. As small farmers were eliminated, the average size of farms increased: and as Irish labor left Ireland, the application of industrial processes to the business of agriculture increased.

Marx argued that the failure of insurrection in 1848 demoralized the Irish peasantry, while the 1853 Act of the British parliament forced the debt-ridden Irish nobility to sell their oft-mortgaged estates. So by the middle of the nineteenth century, Ireland's estates had passed increasingly from their former owners to English capitalist farmers. For Marx and Engels, Ireland's poverty and misery were not as English public opinion would have it, caused by "Irish nature," but rather by English oppression and exploitation.

Regarding the "well known" Irish propensity for crime, Marx pointed to the government's own statistics to disprove this racist myth. In the late 1840s, when economic misery stalked the land, arrests and convictions soared by more than 21,000 crime convictions out of a total of 41,989 arrests in 1849. By 1858, when the economy improved with a rise in the demand for Irish labor (due to the previous massive death and emigration) criminal convictions were only 3,350 out of 6,308 arrests. Marx therefore concluded in an article published in the *Daily Tribune* on September 16, 1859, that poverty was the true cause of most crimes, not the "nature" of the Irish.

Political Infighting

Life in London may have allowed Marx time for calm reflection, research, and writing, but it did not entirely curb his passion for attacks on perceived opponents within the radical movement. In 1852, he took time out from his serious scholarship to write an amusing and very acerbic attack on the exiled leaders from the failed revolutions of 1848–1849. Entitled *Heroes of the Exile*, he dismissed the egotism and conspiratorial fantasies of the former radicals. In essence, he argued that they were incompetents who were saved by the victory of reaction because it "swept them out of the country and made saints and martyrs of them." In fact, he went on to argue that their constant propaganda from abroad was of little practical use to the revolution, and instead it was used as a pretext by repressive German governments to jail radicals and "use these wretched straw men in London as scarecrows with which to frighten the German middle classes."

Marx's analysis is spiced with wonderfully savage put-downs. Joining Marx in his London exile was now former members of the Frankfurt Parliament, the Berlin National Assembly, and Chamber of Deputies. He describes this "hotch-potch" as "writers without a public, loudmouths from the democratic clubs and congresses, twelfth-rate journalists and so forth." These people were the "refuse of mankind," which "found itself hindered by its own impotence as much as by the prevailing situation from undertaking any real action ... [so they] ... indulge in spurious activity whose imagined deeds, imagined parties, imagined struggles and imagined interests have been so noisily trumpeted abroad by those involved." This all makes for delightfully satirical reading, but one wonders if Marx's friends were not right when they warned that he was wasting his talents in such labors. In fact, this and his later obsession with a police agent named Vogt point to one of Marx's less admirable qualities. When someone became an enemy in his mind, Marx would become obsessed with that person even to point of neglecting important work. Instead, he would squander his talent in long polemics of little interest even to his closest allies.

Some years later, Marx was slandered as "the directing and superior head" of a band of blackmailers and forgers. This, along with masses of other insults, was thrown at the London exile by German scientist Karl Vogt. Marx and his friends suspected that Vogt worked for one or another government hostile to their political views. Rather than ignore what most considered a fairly ineffective slander campaign, Marx devoted—most say wasted—the best part of a year writing an incredibly detailed response to Vogt's charges. Few even among his admirers were interested in reading the massive *Herr Vogt* when it was finished in 1860. Since that time, it has seldom been reprinted and even less frequently read. This is as it should be since it is of little importance in terms of theory or history.

The fact that Karl Vogt was revealed ten years later to be in the pay of Napoleon III, dictator of France, does not make this distraction any more appealing as a work of lasting interest. However, the work is something like *Heroes of the Exile*—a marvelous showcase for Marx's biting prose, as when he alludes to

Shakespeare in stating the "original of Karl Vogt is the immortal Sir John Falstaff and in his zoological resurrection he has lost nothing of his character." A clever turn of phrase to be sure but Marx is adding little to his theory by comments such as this.

For all Marx's clever phrases and witty allusions that his friends and comrades appreciated at the time, these political polemics were not the best use of his talent. His situation revealed a cruel dilemma faced by many activist intellectuals. Marx, the intellectual, wished to concentrate on what he regarded as his scientific work and eschew the petty intrigues and uncertain friends that swarm around radical politics. On the other hand, Marx the political animal, found it difficult to suffer fools in silence, particularly when he thought them a danger to the movement. For example, he felt obligated to waste precious time and energy fighting with the anarchist leader, Bakunin, who was alternately either half-mad or half-criminal. Marx judged this fight as necessary to prevent Bakunin and his ilk, including at least one known murderer, from causing great harm to the workers movement.

Regardless of the wisdom of this view, it pulled Marx the thinker down to the level of a petty political actor. The fact is that while many people have at least heard of *Das Kapital* and may even be familiar with some of its main points, few know or care about "Fictitious Splits in the International." Of course, it is impossible to imagine Marx standing aloof from all political fights. That would have reduced him to little more than another unemployed professor. The problem was, as we know from Engels and other friends, that Marx had difficulty in picking fights wisely. To make an extensive critique of the dictator of France, Louis Bonaparte, is completely reasonable. To fight anarchists within the International Working Men's Association might have been an unavoidable political necessity. But, the waste of Marx's time and intellectual efforts on a third-rate police agent like "Herr Vogt" was something else.

Chartism

Not all of Marx's political activities in London had the sad odor that surrounded the Herr Vogt affair. In the 1830s, long before Marx's arrival, a radical working class movement had developed there known to history as the Chartists. Fighting to overcome the British class system by the introduction to universal male democracy, the Chartists held mass meetings and demonstrations throughout the country for decades. The tactic the movement was best known for was to push to gather millions of signatures on petitions that would later be presented to Parliament. These petitions would ask the members of Parliament to pass legislation that would allow peaceful democratic change. Their most famous campaign was for the People's Charter of 1842. This document demanded a democratic restructuring of the British government by means of six seemingly simple reforms: (1) allowing all adult men to vote, (2) have voting be by secret ballot, (3) elimination of property qualifications for Parliament members, (4) salaries for elected representatives, (5) electoral districts representing equal numbers of people, and (6) annually elected Parliaments. Not a list that would raise that many objections from many people in the twenty-first century.

By contrast, the then British government not only rejected the Chartist petitions but also subjected the movement to deep repression with any number of leaders being arrested. Thus, the Chartists were past their peak by the time Marx took up residence in London. All the same, he established relations with the remnants of the movement. A Chartist Conference held in Manchester in March 1854 received a warm letter from Marx. After thanking the congress for offering him a seat as an honorary delegate, he pointed out the tremendous changes that the working masses of Great Britain had caused. He noted that the British "working-classes, with invincible energies, by the sweat of their brows and brains, have called into life the material means of ennobling labor itself, and of multiplying its fruits to such a degree as to make general abundance possible." From this and other writings, it is clear that Marx saw Chartism as the prototype of a modern working class movement.

For their part, the Chartists held Marx in high esteem. As he described in a letter of April 16, 1856, to Engels, at a banquet to celebrate the anniversary of *The People's Paper*, Marx was the only political émigré invited. The honor was confirmed when the first toast was given to Marx who made a short speech in English on the condition it would not be reprinted (and thereby reveal his continuing weakness in that language). From the 1850s onward, both Marx and Engels continued in close contact with Chartist leaders and their movement. It was the Chartist *Red Republican* that published one of the first English translations of the *Communist Manifesto*.

Naturally, there were the inevitable political disagreements. Perhaps most notable was when Marx felt that Chartist icon Ernest Jones had began to flirt with the bourgeoisie. This resulted from Jones having conversations with reformers who wished to soften but not fundamentally change the current social system. Such differences of opinion notwithstanding, Marx and Engels always were favorable to what they saw as an indigenous working class radical movement. Despite their occasional disagreement, when Jones died suddenly in 1869, Marx wrote privately that the longtime Chartist was "one of our few old friends." In fact, Marx and Engels most always keep a soft spot in their heart for the Chartists.

CHAPTER

Workers of the World, Unite:
The International Working
Men's Association (IWMA)

Introduction

After a ten-year period of relative quiet among the working class following the defeat of the revolts throughout Europe of 1848–1849, those who labored for a living began to regain an interest in political activity. As the famous historian Eric Hobsbawm has noted, it was a curious amalgam of "political and industrial action, of various kinds of radicalism from the democratic to the anarchist, of class struggles, class alliances ... inseparable from the international solidarity of the working classes." It was the transnational quality of the labor upsurge that would strike observers, among them Karl Marx.

In 1860, the newly formed London Trades Council organized a mass rally of 50,000 to hail Giuseppe Garibaldi as liberator of Italy. Garibaldi, although remembered more for his passionate nationalism, was a man of the left and, in fact, later became a card-carrying member of the International Working Men's Association (IWMA). That is to say, Garibaldi was firmly on the side of democracy, equality, and the rights of the people. He saw the IWMA as an institution of struggle to help the common people obtain their rights. French workers sent as a delegation by Napoleon III to the Exhibition of 1862 used this visit to make contacts with people such as the secretary of the London Trades Council. At a later meeting at St. James's Hall [March 1863], the Trades Council expressed support for Abraham Lincoln and the fight against the slavery in America. Karl Marx attended this meeting and was very impressed with the workers' speeches opposing slavery. When a number of French workers traveled to London in July 1863 to support freedom for Poland, plans were begun to establish an organization of international solidarity. A meeting was called on September 28, 1864, and the delegates present established an International Working Men's Association.

Establishing the IWMA

Had the organizers only wished for a modest association in order to coordinate communication and strike support between English and French workers, they need not have seized upon such a lofty name that included the adjective "international." Having resolved to make their organization international, the organizers had to have at least symbolic representation beyond the Franco-English delegations. This explains why Victor Le Lubez looked up Karl Marx and asked if he could suggest someone to represent the Germans. Marx nominated an old friend from the Communist League, Johann Georg Eccarius, an émigré tailor. It was to be the involvement of so many genuine workers like Eccarius who attended the inaugural rally that caused Marx to break his general rule of declining to attend political meetings, as he seemingly found them to be a waste of time. Sadly, Eccarius and Marx later had a falling out. There is some evidence that the former may have sold information to the Austrian government. Regardless of the truth of the charge, the fact is that both political splits and police spies were a fact of nineteenth-century European radical life.

He came to St. Martin's Hall only as a silent, if increasingly eager, observer. Yet, Marx's enthusiasm led to him becoming involved in the IWMA. Forgetting the time he needed for his research, writing and ignoring his past unpleasant experience with political organizations, by the end of the evening Karl Marx found himself co-opted onto the General Council of the IWMA. He certainly found himself in strange company. The General Council was overwhelming made up of rather practical-minded English trade union types, as well as French utopians who dreamed of revolution. The former were almost all from the skilled trades and looking for ways to bump up wage levels while on the contrary the latter looked down on trade unionism. Add in some republicans who detested all monarchies, fighters for Polish freedom, and even supporters of the Italian nationalist Mazzini, and it is not a surprise that such a collection could agree on almost nothing. Realizing how much time this would take from *Capital*, Marx at one point tried to cut back on his commitment because he was a "head worker rather than a hand worker." But others on the Council, although generally wary of intellectuals and anyone with less than a working-class pedigree, found him too valuable to let him step back onto the sidelines.

While most office-holders were certainly working class, Karl Marx himself seemed to be unfazed by his rather privileged background. When Engels followed him onto the General Council, it was an even tougher issue given that Frederick had been a successful capitalist rather than merely a poor intellectual. Both would probably have rather stayed out of the limelight but they felt their effort was needed if the IWMA were to survive. Marx threw himself into the work of the IWMA, what has become known as the First International, often dealing with the rather mundane but necessary work that keeps any organization functioning. In a letter of May 1, 1865, to Engels, Marx complained about attempting to finish his own work while "having my time extraordinarily taken up by the 'International Association.'" Later the following year, he commented to Ludwig Kugelmann that he did not wish to attend the Geneva Congress of the IWMA "since such a prolonged interruption of my work is not possible ... this work which I am doing is much more important for the working class than anything I could do personally at a Congress ..."

Of course, he had only himself to blame for this situation because Marx was a bit of a perfectionist. He could not stand by and watch the International issue what he thought were vague or fuzzy proclamations. Thus he found himself writing or editing a vast percentage of the material central to the International. One clear example is how Marx managed to get elected to a subcommittee charged with writing up the rules and principles of the IWMA. Marx, falling ill, missed several meeting only to learn that the group had come up with a badly written and politically inconsistent draft. After a long debate, the draft was sent back to the subcommittee for further editing. Marx could not restrain himself. First, he convinced the subcommittee it would be more comfortable for them to meet at his house. Once there, Marx managed to keep them talking late into the night. Then he modestly suggested he'd try his hand at a draft. The result was that he wrote the rules governing the organization during the stormy years ahead.

Looking at the *General Rules* penned by Marx in October 1864 and adopted the following month by the IWMA, one sees the fingerprints of the author all over the document. It starts by noting that "the emancipation of the working class must be conquered by the working classes themselves ... for equal rights and duties, and the abolition of class rule." Next it goes on to argue that proletarian movements have failed in the past "from want of solidarity" between various groups within each country and the "absence of a fraternal bond of union between the working classes of different countries." To overcome these divisions, the IWMA was founded to recruit those who "will acknowledge truth, justice, and morality as the basis of their conduct toward each other and toward all men, without regard to color, creed or nationality." Both the style and the content owe much to the Marx of the earlier *Communist Manifesto*.

After the preamble, over a dozen specific rules were laid down. The very first one establishes the IWMA's purpose to serve as a "central medium of communication and co-operation" between different groups aiming at the "protection, advancement and complete emancipation of the working classes." Although many of the rules are procedural, they show the hand of Karl Marx and his attempt to provide what he thought was a reasoned response to industrial capitalism. For example, the sixth rule stressed the need for workers to "be consistently informed of the movements of their class in every other country" and for the General Council to "publish periodical reports." The next rule emphasized the necessity of unity between various groups and organizations within each nation. Therefore, the International "shall use their utmost efforts to combine the disconnected workingmen's societies of their respective countries into national bodies." Notably, the tenth rule allowed that members leaving their native country would be helped by IWMA members in their new country. What Marx attempted to put forth in these rules were a number of political concepts. Among the most important were the centrality of the self-emancipation of the working class, the need for unity to combat the ever-growing concentration of capitalist industry, and the global nature of the class struggle.

Spreading the Word

Of great importance was the fact that few people had heard of the International and fewer still knew anything about it. Marx sought to overcome this problem by an extensive outreach program focusing mainly on the printed word—propaganda, if you will. The periodical to first publish the IWMA's documents and reports was the independent trade union weekly *The Bee-Hive*, later known as the *Bee-Hive Newspaper* and the *Penny Bee-Hive*. It was to publish the International's "Rules" in November 1864 and published reports from the IWMA until relations ended in April 1870. Within a year of its foundation, the IWMA could claim five publications as its own. At different times, the International had as many as eighteen supportive publications in cities including Antwerp, Amsterdam, Paris, Barcelona, Madrid, Geneva, Naples, and Brussels.

Some of these had extremely small circulations and lasted only a brief time. Others fell under the influence of a group of anarchists known as the Proudhonists, who were hostile to the General Council. Yet, all boasted of their affiliation with the IWMA and would honor Marx even while rejecting his theories. Besides those official outlets, there was a wealth of labor and socialist papers, magazines, and journals that were friendly to, if independent from, the International. These, including the *Social-Demokrat* in Berlin, could be counted on to give favorable notice to the IWMA's statements and activities. Even so, this still meant that the vast parts of the International's potential followers were unlikely to hear much about it. In order to remedy this, Marx convinced the General Council to seek publication in the mainstream, or bourgeois, press.

On what he considered an enemy terrain, Marx knew he could not always count on a fair, let alone sympathetic, report of IWMA statements and actions. All the same, he felt that it would be foolish to ignore the immense influence and circulation that the mainstream press had. This tactic of seeking coverage from those predisposed to be hostile to the aims of his organization insured much frustration, not to mention a few rages. Still, when the *Times* of London published a document from the International or the *Chicago Tribune* ran an interview with Marx, it seemed worth it. For the most part, Marx felt that the International, or IWMA as it was officially titled, would have to depend on the word-of-mouth promotion from various labor societies and individual radical workers. Further enlightenment was to come from his writings (that often had difficulty seeing the light of day in published form) and the vast amount of correspondence written by both Marx and Engels. In addition to writing to comrades and friends, the two frequently wrote letters of clarification, protest, or information to all sorts of publications. Karl Marx realized the difficulty of his position in promoting the IWMA. While wishing to stay in the background, he was forced by events to take any overly active role. He often thought that his work for the International could never be completed in his lifetime.

In February 1865, Marx met his future son-in-law, Paul Lafargue, who had traveled from Paris to bring news of the International's progress in France. Lafargue liked to tell people that the blood of three oppressed races flowed through his veins. This is a reference to the fact that of his grandparents only one was a white Frenchman. One of his grandmothers was a Jamaican Native American and another was a black refugee from Haiti. His grandfather on his mother's side was a French Jew. Once when asked about his ethnic background, Paul Lafargue promptly responded that he was proudest of his "Negro extraction." Marx often made unflattering comments about this background in private to Engels. Still, he genuinely liked Lafargue, did not object to his marriage to daughter Laura, and, over time, this man of mixed ethnicity became one of Marx's closest political allies and friends.

At his first meeting with Marx, Lafargue, who was only twenty-four years old, was impressed and even a little apprehensive by the already legendary man. Marx took him aside and said, "I must educate men who, after me, will carry on the Communist propaganda." Later, he also confided to Lafargue that he depended on his intellectual partner Engels. The Frenchman soon realized that Engels' opinion was held in higher esteem by Marx than any other individual. Later Lafargue commented that "to win over Engels's opinion was to Marx a triumph."

Marx and the IWMA General Council

Despite his stated reluctance to become immersed in the day-to-day work of the IWMA (or International), Marx's brilliance and energy soon made him the most important member of the General Council. He wrote to Engels in 1865 that, "I am in fact the head of the thing." Marx's friend could not at first understand why Marx spent so much time in meaningless political squabbles and dull administrative work. Engels predicted that the whole thing would not last long. Yet, when he retired to London in 1870, Engels was also compelled to become active in the IWMA, likely against *his* better judgment. Early in his involvement with the International, Marx had written to Engels describing the trivial tasks that took up his time. Tuesday was taken up with the General Council where there were political disputes lasting until midnight. Rather than return home, Marx would retreat to a local bar where he had to sign two hundred IWMA membership cards. Wednesday saw his involvement with a meeting at St. Martin's Hall to mark a Polish uprising. Both Saturday and Monday were devoted to discussions of France at subcommittee meetings. Between and betwixt all these gatherings, Marx was swamped with people who "had to" talk with him about this idea or that project. Much of this activity was in preparation for a conference on suffrage scheduled for the following weekend.

Still, membership on the General Council of the IWMA allowed Marx to become familiar with a number of British trade unionists. Upon having dinner with them, Marx probed these men as to the prevailing pragmatism displayed toward social issues by British organized labor. He always impressed his guests, even if he usually was unable to completely persuade them of his views. His high profile also ensured a steady flow of European radicals, and more than the occasional police spy. Both groups sought him out to better learn his views, albeit with vastly different motivations. All of this activity and attention kept Marx busy, but one wonders if the IWMA ever lived up to his hopes.

Certainly there were some successful campaigns where the IWMA was able to prevent English owners from using foreign laborers to come and take over the jobs of striking workers and thus become "strikebreakers." Soon after becoming organized, London journeymen tailors formed a union and demanded wage increases in line with the rise in the cost of living. The owners hoped to defeat this movement by recruiting journeymen tailors in Belgium, France, and Switzerland. When secretaries of the Central Council of the IWMA put warnings in newspapers in those nations, the owners were defeated for the time being. Writing in March 1865, Marx noted that the attempt to use Scots to undercut London tailors had failed as wages in the industry rose 15 percent in Edinburgh. Then, the bosses secretly "sent agents to Germany to recruit journeymen tailors … for importation to Edinburgh." The International campaign alerted German workers to the situation, knowing that the German tailors were not keen to, in Marx's words, "become *obedient mercenaries of capital* in its struggle against labor."

All the same, the trade unions that signed up with the International tended to be rather marginal, like the Hand-in-Hand Society of Coopers or the English Journeymen Hairdressers. The more powerful industrial unions, such as the Amalgamated Society of Engineers, kept their distance. Even the London Trades Council was aloof, despite the fact that Trades Council leader George Odger was president of the IWMA and secretary to the Council. In order to grow in the directions it aspired to go, the International would have had to bring in more industrial workers.

Lincoln, the American Civil War, and the International

The IWMA, this new International, that Karl Marx helped to pilot soon found itself concerned with affairs far afield from the immediate concerns of the white European workers it had originally been formed to serve. On the world stage, no event loomed larger than Abraham Lincoln's reelection as president in the midst of the American Civil War. The blockade of Confederate (Southern) ports shipping cotton to the mills of England by Lincoln's Union navy was causing economic distress to English cotton producers and by extension the people who worked for them. Under such circumstances, it comes as no surprise that many mill owners and their friends in the British House of Commons were openly supportive of the Confederacy of Southern States, which was a vital supplier of the raw material needed for textile manufacture. The poverty suffered by textile workers was consistently laid by English cloth magnates at the door of Lincoln and the North's wartime policies.

Moreover, British members of Parliament waxed eloquently about the "freedom of the seas" and how Lincoln's government was violating this "sacred principle." In such conditions, a considerable backlash against Lincoln and the Northern federal government would have been far from unexpected from many British workers. Yet, Marx realized the deep sympathy average Britons had for Lincoln, particularly after the Emancipation Proclamation had transformed the Civil War into what many now viewed as a war against slavery. In November 1864, Marx wrote a letter on behalf of the IWMA to Abraham Lincoln, presented to U.S. Ambassador Charles Francis Adams on January 28, 1865. The address congratulated Lincoln on his reelection, noting that "the triumphant war cry of your reelection is Death to Slavery." Not only was the struggle against slavery a cause supported by most workers despite "the hardships imposed on them by the cotton crisis, it was the first act in a drama that would transform the American Republic."

"The workingmen of Europe feel sure," Marx argued, "that, as the American War of Independence initiated a new era of ascendancy for the middle class, so the American anti-slavery War will do for the working classes." Notably, the IWMA address hails Lincoln as "the single-minded son of the working class" [chosen] "to lead his country through the matchless struggle for the rescue of an enchained race and the reconstruction of a social world." Marx elsewhere expanded upon his idea that white labor could never be truly free while black labor was enslaved. IWMA leaders had great hopes for the ramifications of a Northern victory, and they worked to organize boycotts of ships loaded with supplies for the Confederacy. These delays were certainly not as decisive as General Sherman's March to the Sea, but nevertheless contributed to weakening the Southern secessionists.

When the Confederacy surrendered, Marx and his comrades rejoiced. As the news of Lincoln's assassination reached London, the followers of the International mourned. In a letter written in May 1865, the General Council of the IWMA addressed President Andrew Johnson. The bitterness was palatable in the opening paragraph where it was said that, "the demon of the 'peculiar institution' [slavery] for the supremacy of which the South rose in arms would not allow his worshipers to honorably succumb in the open field. What had begun in treason, he must needs end in infamy." In what clearly was later seen wishful thinking, the letter assured Johnson he is destined "to preside over the arduous work of political reconstruction and social regeneration. A profound sense of your great mission will save you from any compromise with stern duties." The letter ended rather naively urging Johnson to "initiate the new era of the emancipation of labor."

If President Johnson turned out to be a disappointment to Marx, and not him alone, the International's excitement at the North's victory was sincere. For the International, and for Marx, the Civil War was a watershed in world history moving rapidly in the direction of a more equal society. For Marx, there was an even more personal connection, as he was in close communication with Joseph Weydemeyer, an old comrade from Prussia. Weydemeyer had been active as the military commander of the St. Louis region and has been credited by some as keeping Missouri from joining the Confederacy, despite the pro-Southern sympathies of rural whites. For many progressive German immigrants who fought for the North, Marx's proclamations confirmed how they felt.

For a time, Marx, influenced by Weydemeyer's letters, believed that the victory of the Union might allow socialism to peacefully evolve in the United States. Writing from St. Louis, Marx's friend argued that an alliance of Northern white workers and freed African Americans could command a majority at elections and transform the Republican Party into a radical party or replace it with a Labor Party. This electoral majority would be able to overcome the power of entrenched economic interests and reshape the United States, democratically, into a social republic. This scheme underestimated white racism and the entrenched power of the established order. Further, it assumed that many old political structures would be eliminated in the course of Reconstruction. With the failure of radical reconstruction and the later disenfranchisement of African American males, these hopes faded.

Marx had also thought that the unfolding Industrial Revolution that followed the Civil War would establish the preconditions for a new society. Exploited workers, who possessed the vote, would support parties who would curb the excesses of the capitalist system. Over time, the industrial system would be replaced by a democratic socialist system. Marx clearly miscalculated. He underestimated the ability of the new industrial elite to manipulate politics to their benefit. He did not understand the depth of anti-African American prejudice, particularly in the South but in the North as well. What Marx thought would become a democratic alternative to Europe with its elitist rule and restricted franchises became instead a supremely successful system of industrial capitalism. In many ways, the United States highlighted the ambiguous nature of Marx's view of the Industrial Revolution. On the one hand, the United States was the great industrial success Marx had predicted. Still, it refused to transform its social or economic system to correspond to the new level of productive forces. He deplored the human cost of the new industrial transformation while, at the same time, contending it built an economic basis for a society that could be equitable, just, and democratic.

The Franco-Prussian War (1870–1871)

Otto von Bismarck, the "Iron Chancellor" of Prussia, realized that a war with an external foe would allow him to whip up feelings necessary to unify the diverse German states into one nation. France, led by the vain and corrupt dictator Emperor Napoleon III, was the perfect candidate to be that enemy. Living off past glory and exaggerated boasting about current strength gave France the illusion of being a mighty power. Bismarck knew this position to be false and proceeded to manipulate a relatively minor diplomatic dispute into a crisis. The provoked French emperor fell into the trap by declaring war against Prussia on July 19, 1870. By the end of the brief war, Germany would emerge as a powerful, united country while France would be plunged into civil war.

The day the war began, Marx conferred with others on the IWMA General Council as to what the organization's response should be. Marx was assigned to write a public address on the nature of the war and how workers should respond to the conflict. By July 23, he had written a draft the "First Address of the International on the Franco-Prussian War," submitted to the secretaries responsible for individual countries on the General Council. Within a short time, the complete General Council approved Marx's work and 30,000 copies in French and German were distributed by the IWMA. Marx appealed to workers on both sides to stand clear of the war and the chauvinism it unleashed. While this plea often fell on deaf ears, two of Marx's allies in the North German Reichstag, German labor leaders August Bebel and Wilhelm Liebknecht, went to jail rather than vote for funds for the war. Marx was also pleased to hear that this address had been praised by the eminent British intellectual John Stuart Mill. On a less cheerful note, Marx and Engels feared that if the German onslaught slowed, Bismarck might call upon the troops of his eastern ally, the Russian Tsar.

The French army collapsed far too easily for the "Russian hordes" to be needed as back up. By September 4, 1870, a Third Republic had been proclaimed and a provisional government was established. Marx hurriedly penned a Second Address that aimed its main criticism against Bismarck and Prussian militarism along with the German bourgeoisie. He argued, in the name of the International, that the annexation of Alsace-Lorraine would set the stage for a future European-wide war. In this future war, Russia might choose to side with France. This Second Address pleaded with the German workers to do everything in their limited power to stop the annexations. Demonstrations and protests were held by responsive Germans, but the Imperial government unleashed a very effective wave of repression in reply. Moreover, as Marx noted in this same document,

> The German working class has resolutely supported the war, which it was not in their power to prevent, as a war for German independence and the liberation of France and Europe from that pestilential incubus, the [French] Second Empire. It was the German workmen who, together with the rural laborers, furnished the sinews and muscles of heroic hosts, leaving behind their half-starved families. Decimated by the battles abroad, they will be once more decimated by misery at home.

If the response from German workers did not support Marx's position, the situation in France was more complex. The war had brought forward strong nationalistic feelings that were further inflamed by the rapid collapse of Napoleon III's army. The International, centered in London, was dominated by its heavily German General Council. This fact allowed Marx's foes, most of all the Russian Bakunin and his anarchist followers, to suggest that the International was on the side of Prussia and that Marx might even be Bismarck's agent. Anyone even slightly aware of the proclamations issued by the IWMA since the beginning of the war, or the personality of Marx, knew this to be false, but in the emotional chaos following France's defeat some were prepared to at least listen to these false charges. By the first month of 1871, Paris was forced to surrender to Bismarck's army after months of siege. On January 18, the Prussian King Wilhelm was proclaimed Kaiser of Germany at the palace of the French monarchy at Versailles. German terms were harsh, including the annexation of Alsace and Lorraine by the new Reich in addition to a huge cash payment from France. It appeared a complete victory for Bismarck and for reactionary nationalism. Then on March 18, 1871, the red flag was to be seen flying over the Paris City Hall.

The Commune of Paris (March 18–May 28, 1871)

Marx had been glad to see a new republic proclaimed in France to replace the hated Emperor Napoleon III but was deeply afraid that the presence of monarchists and other antidemocratic elements in the provisional government might result in the restoration of monarchy. Nonetheless, he urged French workers and most particularly members of the IWMA to support the new republic and work within it to achieve their goals. As he pleaded in the Council's Second Address, "Any attempt at upsetting the new government in the present crisis, when the enemy is almost knocking at the doors of Paris, would be a desperate folly. The French workmen must perform their duties as citizens." Moreover, in the name of the IWMA, Marx urged looking beyond the present crisis. French workers "have not to recapitulate the past, but to build up the future. Let them calmly and resolutely improve the opportunities of republican liberty, for the work of their own class organization." Unfortunately, the common people of Paris, even members of IWMA, ignored Marx's advice.

Parisians, already furious at their nation's defeat at the hands of Bismarck, were beside themselves when the new republic announced that reparations to Berlin would be paid by the immediate collection of all outstanding bills and rents previously suspended during the siege of Paris. When, on March 18, 1871, all weapons including cannons paid for by public subscription were ordered to be handed over, an angry crowd took to the streets. Backed by the Paris National Guard, the revolt was of such magnitude that France's capital was left in the hands of the common people, and soon afterward most of the rich fled to Versailles. If this were to be a successful revolution, Marx noted that the people should have immediately marched on Versailles and seized the wealth of the Bank of France. In a word, Marx urged decisive action. Instead, they held elections for a new democratic government. Although only men could vote, it is interesting that the question of female voting was seriously discussed in the weeks that followed.

On the next morning, Paris found itself free of the old order. The real power was now in the hands of the leadership of the Paris National Guard. During the course of the war with the Germans, the Paris National Guard had become composed of average Parisians rather than professional soldiers and politicians. Among the leadership were fifteen socialists of various hues claiming membership in the International. Rather than consolidate their power, the National Guard handed it over to the people of Paris by calling for an election of communal representatives on March 22. This election was opposed by various conservative forces such as Deputies to the National Assembly living in Paris. These men wanted the newly proclaimed conservative government headquartered at Versailles to be the sole legitimate power.

When elections were held, ninety-two Communards were elected including seventeen members of the IWMA. Most of the others chosen by the voters were Radical or Jacobin types with only a few respectable people elected who soon resigned in disgust. The whole Commune government, out of necessity, found that it had to wholeheartedly support the common people even when this meant the infringement of property rights. With most of the conservative, wealthy, or other opponents of the Commune having left Paris, the population that remained was dominated by workers, more often craftsmen than industrial laborers, and small property owners.

The measures that this short-lived, local government passed are all the more remarkable given the almost complete lack of preparation or political agreement among the very mixed bag of political actors in Paris in those days. Among other things, the Commune of Paris abolished conscription and the standing army, replacing it with the "people in arms" through the vehicle of the Paris National Guard. It imposed a rent freeze and stopped the sale of all items pledged in city own pawnshops. The Commune set the salary of government officials at no more than that which an average person would make. Complete separation of church and state was legislated, with all religious instruction and symbols to be excluded from schools. Closed factories were to be re-opened and run as worker cooperatives. Foreigners were given the same rights as the native French, as

"the flag of the Commune is the flag of the World Republic." Specific griev-
ances were addressed as exemplified by the Commune abolishing night work
for bakers. At other times, the measures were more of a symbolic nature such as
ordering the demolition of the Chapel of Atonement, which had been erected as
an apology for the execution of King Louis XVI.

Clearly, the IWMA was far from the dominant force that enemies would later
claim. In London, it was decided that Marx should write an "address to the People of Paris." Sadly, Marx was in little condition to fulfill this obligation. During a large part of April and May, Marx was ill and was unable to attend
meetings of the General Council, let alone gather his wits to analyze the com-
plexity of the Commune's experience. When at the end of May, Marx delivered
his masterful *Civil War in France*; the Commune had already been crushed
some days before by French government troops sent by the bourgeois government of the Third Republic, with tens of thousands of Communards paying with
their blood for their beliefs.

During this period of ill health, Marx still managed to write countless letters
calling upon English, American, Austrian, and German workers to organize solidarity rallies and actions in defense of the Commune. After the fall of the Paris
Commune, August Bebel rose in the German Reichstag (Congress) and told the
assembled representatives of the status quo that the "entire proletariat of Europe" was watching Paris. Further, the German socialist leader predicted that
"before many decades go by, the battle-cry of the Parisian proletariat, 'War
against the palaces, peace for the huts of the poor, an end to poverty and para-
sites!' will become the battle-cry of the entire European working class."

Marx drew numerous lessons from the Paris Commune and its brief history.
The Commune, Marx argued, proved that the working class cannot simply take
over an existing state apparatus. Rather, it must create a new series of structures
consistent with their class goals and political ideals. Thus, the Commune had
rapidly dissolved the old political police, had replaced the professional army by
the people in arms, freed schools from religious and political interference, and
introduced the elective principle into the public service including members of
the judiciary. The idea was a democracy where all who served would be responsible to those that elected them and could be removed at any time should their
performance disappoint their electors. Later, Engels would point to the Paris
Commune as the first example of the "Dictatorship of the Proletariat." Still
Marx, for all his seemingly limitless enthusiasm for the achievements of
the short-lived democratic experiment that was the Commune, understood its
limitations.

A decade later, when answering a Dutch socialist who asked what measures a
worker's state should take upon coming to power, Marx commented,

> Perhaps you will point to the Paris Commune; but apart from the fact that
> this was merely the rising of a town under exceptional conditions, the majority
> of the Commune was in no sense socialist, nor could it be. With a small amount
> of sound common sense, however, they could have reached a compromise with
> Versailles useful to the whole mass of the people—the only thing that could be

reached at the time. The appropriation of the Bank of France alone would have been enough to dissolve all the pretensions of the Versailles people in terror ... [the problem is that] doctrinaire and necessarily fantastic anticipations of the program of action for a revolution of the future only divert us from the struggle of the present.

Above all else, Marx knew that the Commune had failed to establish itself outside of Paris in any meaningful way. It seemed able to govern itself but did not take seriously enough the furious blows that would inevitably rain down upon it from the bourgeois government at Versailles. This doomed the noble experiment to isolation and ultimate destruction.

Marx's *Civil War in France* proved to be one of his finest, and most popular, works. The first printing numbered around 3,000 and was quickly sold, with French and German translations quickly following. *The Civil War in France* wound up creating quite a stir. Two moderate English trade union members left the IMWA's General Council and began their walk down the well-worn path of Liberal Party politics. For much of the mainstream press, the Commune was identified with murder, looting, and arson, the facts not withstanding. Given the limited media open to Marx and the International, these distortions were reported far more often than the true story of the Commune.

The position Marx articulated on behalf of the IWMA gave added employment opportunities for police spies as every member of the General Council found themselves closely watched. When Marx left for a seaside vacation in August 1871, he found himself with a shadow in the form of a police agent lurking in the promenades. Confiding to his wife, Marx tells how he rid himself of the pest: "Yesterday the thing got to be a bore. I stopped, turned about and fixed a look on the fellow through the notorious eyeglass. What did he do? He removed his hat very humbly and has today no longer favored me by following me about."

That same summer, Marx's daughters Jenny and sixteen-year-old Eleanor visited their married sister Laura Lafargue in southern France. After the defeat of the Commune, Paul Lafargue had gone into hiding and in hopes of discovering his location, the police arrested the Marx sisters, forced them to submit to a strip search, and threw them into a gendarme's police barracks. Jenny had a letter in her pocket from a leader of the Commune. Had it been found, both Marx sisters may have been sent for a lengthy stretch in a French penal colony like that in New Caledonia. Luckily, the officer left the women alone for in his office for a moment. Jenny quickly opened a dusty old account book and stuffed the incriminating letter inside. Joking, Engels once said it may still be in that book.

Failing to force either Jenny or Eleanor to inform on their brother-in-law or admit any other political transgression, the police finally had to release them without charges. The quick thinking Jenny later went on to marry Charles Longuet, a former member of the Commune. While the Marx sisters were released, thousand of other political prisoners were not. The fact was that stern repression destroyed the French section of the IWMA for all intents and purposes. Things went little better with other sections, since identification with the Commune frightened more timid reformers, while it attracted anarchists.

Struggle with Bakunin and Anarchism

A greater problem in some ways than police oppression was the increased activity of Bakunin and his anarchist followers in the IWMA. Bakuninists steadfastly interpreted the events of the Paris Commune as proving the validity of anarchism. This was in complete opposition to the interpretation of Marx, Engels, and most of the IWMA General Council. For the latter, the Paris Commune proved that a state, a people's state but a state all the same, was necessary for the social revolution. Meanwhile, Bakunin was willfully blind to any of the various evidences of political organization that took place during the Commune's brief existence. On the other side, Marx had pointed to the fall of the Communards as resulting from insufficient organization and revolutionary clarity, such as not seizing the Bank of France when the opportunity presented itself. While the anarchists proclaimed their rejection of any activity "that did not have as its immediate and direct aim the triumph of the cause of the workers against capital," Marx calmly argued that revolutions are not made, but develop out of ripening social conditions. For him, the most important thing that can be done to ensure their future success is to prepare the workers for the next revolutionary crisis so that when it appears, they will not miss their chance. Anarchists, for their part, refused to support gradual steps or transitional periods during which a government or state might remain. They felt that all structures of the old order had to be destroyed at once rather than modified or transformed.

The dispute with the anarchists would have been bad enough even if it had taken place in a relatively civil atmosphere. Worse yet, Marx and Bakunin, who had known each other since 1843, grew ever more bitter and hostile to each other as the struggle for control of the IWMA developed. While Bakunin claimed to respect the scientific work done by Marx and his followers, he claimed they "poison the atmosphere. Vanity, malevolence, gossip, pretentiousness and boasting in theory and cowardice in practice. Dissertations about life, action and feeling and complete absence of life, action and feeling." Meanwhile, Marx referred to Bakunin in a letter to Friedrich Bolte on November 23, 1871, as "a man devoid of theoretical knowledge, ... [for whom theory] is a secondary affair—merely a means to his personal self-assertion. If he is a nonentity as a theoretician he is in his element as an intriguer." The Russian anarchist took the view that Marx and his followers slander their opponents with "the epithet BOURGEOIS! [it] is shouted *ad nauseam* by people who are from head to foot more bourgeois than anyone in a provincial city—in short, foolishness and lies. Lies and foolishness."

The growing split in the IWMA was taking place on a regional basis. Marx argued that Bakunin's program was an "infants' spelling-book [that] found favor (and still has a certain hold) in Italy and Spain, where the real conditions of the workers' movement are as yet little developed, and among a few, vain, ambitious and empty doctrinaires in French Switzerland and Belgium." In other words, anarchism was only strong in countries or regions that had not been significantly touched by the Industrial Revolution. Increasingly, Marx and his followers dismissed anarchism and Bakunin as the last gasp of dying rural societies as opposed to the industrialized countries that were creating an ever-growing working class and thus the basis for socialism.

To the twenty-first century mind, the dispute between Karl Marx and the anarchists might appear like a clash of egos fighting over obscure points of ideology. Of course, there was some of that as Bakunin and Marx, not to mention Engels, had very healthy egos. Yet, the fact is that there was, and is, a fundamentally divergent reaction to the Industrial Revolution beneath all the bickering. Karl Marx, we must remember, saw industrialism as a potentially vast advance for all of humanity. The revolution in the way things were produced, according to Marx, could establish the economic basis for a society where people were spared the worst of toil while machines increasingly did the work previously forced upon humans. This had the potential to lead to a society where people were, finally, free from the limitations necessity had always placed upon them.

The problem was, said the authors of the *Communist Manifesto*, that a small class of property owners appropriated the benefits mainly to themselves. This bourgeois would even hold back technology if it helped protect their profits. The solution to Marx and his supporters was a revolution that would give the people the power to harness the Industrial Revolution to human needs rather than to profit. Thus, the idea was not to destroy or resist industrialism per se but rather redirect it to fulfill human needs and desires. In politics, this meant not the immediate elimination of the state but the creation of a government that was completely democratic. The new society must hold elections for every position of power, Marx argued after the experience of the Paris Commune. Over time, as increasing equality eliminated the basis for conflict, crime, and war, the repressive features of government (politics, the army, jails) would "wither away." The state of governmental apparatus would more and more focus on tasks like delivering the mail or building public transportation.

For Marx, the problem was never individuals but the way society was organized. He saw state problems as the result of imperfect systems rather than evil individuals. Often, he pointed out that as individuals, capitalists might be the nicest of people but the system of ruthless competition obligated them to act in a ruthless manner or be swept aside. Not surprisingly, this vision of social change struck a chord in industrializing societies that saw both the benefits and the problems of this new system of production. Therefore, the popularity of Marx in Germany had more to do with an industrial history where Marx's ideas made sense rather than any mere nationalistic attachment to a native German.

By contrast, Bakunin and his followers rejected the Industrial Revolution and even political democracy. Strongest in the agricultural regions of Europe, Bakunin dreamed of a world without industrialization or government. Instead of taming the ravages of the industrial system or redirecting it onto a new path,

Bakunin wanted to go backward to a world of self-sufficient farmers and craftsmen. While Marx saw the Industrial Revolution as potentially liberating but subject to abuse by the greedy, most anarchists saw only the evil in this new mode of production. Their position may sound odd but it was the perspective of the shoe maker impoverished by shoe factories and peasants displaced by industrialized agriculture. Many of these people wanted to return to an idealized past. Likewise in politics, Bakunin saw the state—government of any sort—as irredeemably evil. It could not be replaced by more fully democratic institutions as "free elections eliminate neither masters nor slaves." (Reformers, of course, were worse than worthless as they just bred illusions.) In many ways, Bakunin and his supporters wanted not freedom *of* politics but freedom *from* politics.

Flowing from this conception, Bakunin wanted the state to be destroyed at once. In place of political struggles, there would be "propaganda of the deed" where heroic persons would assassinate evil politicians and bosses. This example, anarchists felt, would one day spark a spontaneous revolt by the masses. To Marx, the only thing such behavior would spark is increased police repression with anarchist actions being used as an excuse to suppress socialists. Like Marx, Engels also argued that individual violence played into the hands of the status quo. Bakunin held firm to his belief that violence was the midwife of a better society. Anarchists thought that if the old society was destroyed, a new and superior one would spontaneously arise. They abused the socialists for their emphasis on organization and education. Karl Marx viewed all these anarchist beliefs as more than wrong. He saw them as reactionary while thinking their actions would not move humanity forward to a better society, something that could only come about with, not against, the Industrial Revolution. In a way, it could be said Marx was for reformed industrialism and democratic socialist politics, while Bakunin rejected both the Industrial Revolution and all government, whether run by the people with the goal of socialism or not.

Death of the First International

With the end of the Paris Commune, the IWMA began to unravel. The best of its French members were dead or in exile. Meanwhile, English trade unionists began to warm to the idea of joining the British Liberal Party and working within the parliamentary system. In the United States, a number of sections of the International were taken over by various unorthodox individuals who advocated, among other things, spiritualism, prohibition, and free love. Tellingly, one leading American IWMA leader was Victoria Woodhull who had started out as a snake oil saleswoman in a traveling medicine show. Lurking in the background was Bakunin who, in the words of one author, "observed the wounded and limping International like a hungry hyena eyeing up its lunch." A special conference held in London in September 1871 saw Marx attempting to control the increasingly unruly anarchist bloc. Although Bakunin was let off lightly, this in no way diminished the Russian's sectarian anger against his political enemies.

In the following months, not only did Bakunin hold his own conference packed with his supporters, but he became increasingly abusive if not unhinged. IWMA members in Italy and Spain received circular letters, in which Bakunin claimed he was being persecuted by "German and Russian Jews." It does Marx and Engels no credit that they would resort to ethnic slurs in their personal correspondence. The way they listed the ethnic background of friend and foe alike as shorthand for their weaknesses may well shock the contemporary reader. Yet, put these things in the context of nineteenth-century discourse and whatever personal prejudices they may have shared with their society, neither man supported racism politically or was a racist. Marx was a Jew by heritage, a Lutheran by baptism, and an atheist by conviction. His attitude can best be summed up by the words of August Bebel, "anti-Semitism is the socialism of fools." In fact, Marx and the IWMA were frequently attacked precisely for "accepting anyone."

By contrast, Bakunin claimed that only the "Latin" race [*sic*] could stop this conspiracy of the "whole Jewish world which constitutes a single parasite, voracious, organized in itself" led by "Marx on the one hand and ... the Rothschilds on the other." Sadly, this prefigures the argument made by the Nazis and other rightist anti-Semites that Jews are involved in a conspiracy ranging from radicals to bankers and ultimately was used to justify genocide. Although anti-Semitism was common in nineteenth-century Europe, this was clearly over the top even for a descendant of the Russian nobility like Bakunin. When the Russian anarchist openly called for a massacre of Jews in a letter to an Italian section of the IWMA, Marx, Engels, and the rest of the General Council had had enough.

In June 1872, a booklet written by Marx entitled *The Fictitious Splits in the International* accused Bakunin of inciting racial hatred and organizing secret societies to wreck the working-class movement. To settle matters once and for all, a Congress was called for September 1872 to be held in The Hague in the Netherlands. Sixty-five delegates attended but so too did scores of reporters, police spies, and the simply curious. Although one newspaper noted that the dangerous Dr. Marx looked like a "gentleman," store owners barred their windows, and one press report even urged women and children to hide in their homes. To contain what was on the verge of becoming a circus, the IWMA Congress went into a closed session to check delegate's credentials. Marx could depend on the French and German delegates, as well as a "Spanish" delegate who turned out to be Marx's French son-in-law Paul Lafargue. The resourceful Lafargue had somehow gotten himself a mandate from Spain despite the solidly pro-Bakunin nature of the delegation.

After a chaotic three days during which Marx and Engels took part personally, as opposed to the absent Bakunin who let his followers fight for his views, it was clear that Marx and the General Council had a majority. On the evening of September 5, the International Congress opened the doors to the public once more. The hall was crowded with more people than it was built to hold, a sure way of furthering the chaos surrounding the debates. The first major vote resulted in the General Council, of which Marx was the leading member, receiving more power than it had previously. The real surprise was when Engels rose to address the assembly. He proposed, with the full support of Marx, that the headquarters of the International leave London for New York. The delegates were stunned. The vote to move the General Council to the far shores of North America received barely a majority.

Marx and Engels argued that increased police repression in Europe, disruptive disputes plaguing the IWMA, and the growing strength of American labor all pointed to the wisdom of such a move. Still, they must have known that they were condemning the organization to death. It appears that even before The Hague Congress, Marx and Engels had decided to end their active involvement. Neither man saw the organization as worth the endless energy it required from them, and they feared that it might fall into the violent hands of men like Bakunin. There was, also, the danger that the Blanquists would gain a majority in the leadership and turn the International toward conspiratorial methods. The followers of the French radical, Louis Auguste Blanqui, appeared to live by the idea that "today is a fine day to overthrow the government." That is, they saw revolution as an insurrectionist act of will rather than as the outcome of a patient process of political organizing. Marx and Engels, however much they may have admired the Blanquists' spirit, thought revolution was too serious a project to be left to small groups of adventurers. Both felt it was better to give the International a dignified death. As Engels put it in a letter to August Bebel in 1873, "knowing that the bubble must burst some time all the same, our concern was not to delay the catastrophe but to take care that the International emerged from it pure and unadulterated."

One important consideration was that Marx may have felt he had insufficient energy. It would be better, he reasoned, to devote himself to finishing the multiple volumes planned for *Capital*. This was particularly the case since there was no longer a united outlook among members of the General Council. With many British trade unionists losing interest and increasing conflicts with Bakunin, Marx thought that the International had accomplished all it could. With the move to New York, the IWMA would stop being a constant distraction for Marx. As Marx had respect for a number of American socialists, he may have even harbored hopes that comrades in North America would be able to have some success. Most of all, both Marx and Engels were tired and believed that European workers had been introduced to the basic ideas of socialism and that was all one could expect to achieve under the circumstances.

To tidy up matters, Marx produced a damning letter that showed Bakunin, involved with an act of potential political violence, conspiring to threaten a publisher with death. So, on the last day of the Congress, by a vote of twenty-seven to seven, Bakunin was expelled from the IWMA.

First International in the United States

If Marx had any hopes for the renewed success of the newly relocated International, they were to end in disappointment within a year of the Hague Congress. For whatever other virtues the United States of America might have possessed, reinvigorating the IWMA was not among them. At first, this was not apparent. Marx and Engels convinced their friend Friedrich Adolph Sorge, whom they had great faith in, to run matters upon his return to New York. Although he had initially opposed moving the International's headquarters from London, Sorge dutifully accepted his new duties as general secretary. He had shown his worth by breaking out of the German immigrant community in America and actually recruiting some U.S. unions to join the IWMA, and seemed able to raise money, which had always been in desperately short supply.

So, the last hope for the IWMA was to lie in the American Republic, where new forces were to be recruited. This soon proved to be a vain hope. The General Council led by Sorge soon found itself isolated from the working class and radical movements everywhere except in the United States. From the beginning, money remained a particular obstacle as with the notable exceptions of Germany, Austria, the Netherlands, and the United States as most sections failed to pay their dues or even contribute significant funds. As prospects faded, the only possibility of a rebirth lay in the next general congress set to convene in Geneva on September 8, 1873. Although the General Council in New York City spent a great amount of effort on calling this meeting, there was insufficient money to allow American delegates to travel to Europe and participate. In the end, the congress was also devoid of delegates from most nations, with the majority of those attending being Swiss, indeed largely from Geneva.

Little life was now left in the IWMA. It limped forward with little left save the formal burial. "The fiasco of the Geneva Congress was inevitable," noted Marx, "once it was clear that not a single delegate from New York would be able to attend, we realized the game was up." It was clear by the latter part of 1873 that neither Marx nor Engels held out any hope (if they ever truly had) that the International would survive on North American soil. Writing to Sorge on September 27, 1873, Marx argued that the International should be allowed to retire into the background so that, at very least, reactionaries would not use the IWMA to attack the left "if all the good bourgeois believe that this bogey has been decently buried." When on July 15, 1876, the last congress of the IWMA was held in Philadelphia with a mere two dozen participants, the delegates unanimously adopted a resolution that the IWMA should be dissolved for an indefinite period.

After the move to America, the IWMA went into quick decline and was officially dissolved in 1876. Bakunin, who wrote of the need for "lies, cunning, entanglement and, if necessary, violence towards enemies," died that same year. The International had passed away but the beliefs that brought about its birth continued.

CHAPTER 5

Das Kapital and the Economics of Industrialism

Introduction

It would be wrong to see Karl Marx as someone who spent all his time involved in an endless series of political brawls and pointless sectarian infighting. As a serious scholar, he set for himself the task in his work *Das Kapital*, or in English *Capital*, of laying "bare the economic law of motion of modern society." In this ambitious undertaking, he was to spend many of the best years of his adult life. He could have contented himself with a briefer, less academic book like his *Wage Labor and Capital* (1847). Marx was, however, more than a bit of a perfectionist so he insisted on research, always more research. Then again, as noted previously, he let himself get distracted by petty political arguments. Writing to Ludwig Kugelmann in 1862, Marx explains the long delay in the appearance of *Das Kapital* in part to "a great deal of my time in 1860 [being] taken up with the Vogt rumpus, since I had a lot of research to do on material which was in itself of little interest, besides engaging in lawsuits, etc."

Moreover, Jenny, his wife, noted in a letter to Berta Markheim in 1863 that Marx would have finished *Capital* long ago if he had kept to his original plan. "But since the Germans really believe only in 'fat' books," Mrs. Marx concluded, "and the far more subtle concentration and elimination of all that is superfluous counts for nothing in the eyes of those worthies, Marx has added a lot more historical material ..." The result was that the first volume of *Capital* was all Marx was to finish on his own. It was left to Engels to put together the next two volumes from Marx's notes. Likewise, Marx's friend was left to finish the three volumes *Theories of Surplus Value* which contains the only draft of the final fourth volume of *Capital*.

The approach taken by Marx toward the Industrial Revolution was twofold. On the one side, he hailed it as the forerunner to humanity's deliverance from the horrors of the past. On the other hand, Marx points to the tremendous suffering that was and is caused by industrialism as it sweeps away all old crafts, habits, and institutions. True to the dialectical method he had inherited from Hegel, he was able to examine both the upsides of the revolution in production while attacking the downside of industrialism under a system dominated by the never-ending search for profit. As early as 1846, in *The German Ideology*, Marx had argued that a "development of the productive forces is the absolutely necessary practical premise [for a socialist society], because without it want is generalized, and with want the struggle for necessities begins again, and that means that all the old crap must revive." By that old crap, Marx meant inequality, exploitation, and class oppression.

While basing much of his economic research on the works of the classical British political economists from Adam Smith's *Wealth of Nations* (1776) through David Ricardo's *Political Economy* (1821), he felt that these thinkers could not get out of their "bourgeois skin" to realize the capital-labor relationship was not a law of nature but rather the result of a historical mode of production. In addition, since the bourgeoisie felt threatened by the revolutions since 1830, they had abandoned science. Marx argues that this fear "sounded the death-knell of scientific bourgeois economy. It was thenceforth no longer a question whether this theorem or that was true, but whether it was useful or harmful. In place of disinterested enquirers there were hired prizefighters."

Commodities, Value, and Money

The economic analysis that follows in the pages of *Capital* can be very challenging, especially for those without classic economical training. Many, many books and articles have been written interpreting this tome in any number of different ways. Some authors have even suggested that, in order to truly understand *Capital*, one must read the chapters in a completely different order from the manner that the author had originally arranged them. Nonetheless, certain key ideas are worth discussing to allow at least a taste of the Marxian economic method. In the very first chapter, Marx discusses commodities and their value. A commodity is something which can be bought and sold. Not only are commodities fundamental units of capitalism, they are, at the same time, objects that satisfy human needs and wants.

For Marx, the commodity possesses a dual value. It has use-value in as much as the commodity may be necessary to satisfy some human need or desire. It also has exchange-value, which is its value in relation to other commodities. This latter value is somewhat independent from the original use-value. Why? Because exchange value is a relation between other commodities in the market with little or no regard for the inherent use-value of a commodity. All value is created by human labor, contends the author of *Capital*, yet what "confirms them in this view, is the peculiar circumstance that the use-value of objects is realized without exchange, by means of a direct relation between the objects and man, while, on the other hand, their value is realized only by exchange, that is, by means of a social process."

Discussing money as part of the circulation of commodities, Marx deals with two elements. He sees money as a measure of value, which is the socially recognized incarnation of human labor. At the same time, money is the standard of price, as it is a fixed weight of precious metal. Marx's formula for the circulation of commodities is: C-M-C, which means a commodity is transformed into money, and then it is transformed back into a commodity. Money is the medium not just of exchange but also of class relations. Marx points to the ancient world where the class struggle "took the form chiefly of a contest between debtors and creditors, which in Rome ended in the ruin of plebeian debtors. They were displaced by slaves." For Marx, money-relations only reflect "the deeper-lying antagonism between the general economic conditions of existence of the classes in question."

If C-M-C represents the formula for commodity circulation, M-C-M shows the transformation of money into capital. In the early C-M-C transactions, money serves only as a medium of exchange. One starts out with let us say apples and by using money as a means of exchange transforms it into some different commodity, maybe oranges. One is, as Marx puts it, selling in order to buy. M-C-M is the true capitalist formula, as one is buying commodities with the aim of reselling them at a higher price, which is to realize a profit. For this exchange to be successful there needs to be a commodity "whose use-value possesses the peculiar property of being a source of value."

Money begets more money because labor-power is uniquely able to produce use-value far beyond the exchange-value "price" paid by the capitalist. The worker produces more value than the socially necessary labor time required reproducing the laborer. "What really influenced [the capitalist] was the specific use-value which this commodity [labor power] possesses of being *a source not only of value, but of more value than it has itself.* This is the special service." Marx argues "that the capitalist expects from labor-power, and in this transaction he acts in accordance with the 'eternal laws' of the exchange of commodities. The seller of labor-power, like the seller of any other commodity, realizes its exchange-value, and parts with its use-value." In other words, the capitalist takes raw materials and uses worker's labor-power to process and infuse these materials with greater use-value, and then sells the finished product for a profit.

Commodities and Fetishism

While commodities are the product of the human mind and produced by human labor, they become fetishes in a capitalist society. A fetish in the Europe of the Middle Ages was an object venerated for its allegedly supernatural powers. One common example of this would be the bones of a saint. The relations of different commodities appear autonomous in a capitalist market and thus according to Marx take on a bizarre transformation akin to the fetishism of medieval Christianity. Marx thought that people failed to understand that the exchange-value of a commodity was determined by the market, and not based on any inherent use-value of the item. One of the main problems with all of this for Karl Marx was his belief that relations between people assume "the fantastic form of a relation between things."

In the contemporary world, a particularly extreme form of fetishism is "branding," whereby a relatively common article of apparel becomes "special" if it is marked with the brand name of a famous designer. Under capitalism, fetishism is the idea that commodities have some inherent value. At times, this fetishism takes forms much like that of the Middle Ages as when people pay hundreds of thousands of dollars for Elvis Presley's belongings.

The Labor Theory of Value

The analysis put forth by Marx is based on the "labor theory of value." That is, that the price of a commodity depends upon the amount of labor that went into producing it. In this, Marx is basing himself on the theories of the classical economist David Ricardo. However, where Ricardo used this theory as a means to attempt to justify the capitalist system of prices, Marx's focus is in unmasking modern industrial capitalism as something other than it presents itself. He suggests that prices and exchange-value are based on the amount of labor used to process the item, and the capitalist makes profit by paying the workers less than the value they produce. Therefore, how the economy is organized has drastic consequence for society. Since modern industrial capitalism is based on private ownership of the means of production, it reduces the common people to a dependent mass forced to sell their labor-power in order to survive. At the same time, the capitalists may own factories, land, and raw materials, but without wage workers producing commodities they would be unable to realize profits.

The ultimate result of this situation is that the social process that produces commodities rests on the exploitation of the worker. If workers were paid the full value of what they produce, there would be no profit. Among the various social consequences of this is the rise of a class struggle between owners and workers. Simply put, the industrialists want workers who will work as long as possible for the least pay. On the other hand, the worker wishes to limit the hours of work while receiving a "fair wage," which normally means more than the owner desires to pay. Many modern economists reject the labor theory of value as outdated but have difficulty dismissing Marx's main argument on the social imbalance of industrial production and the resulting class antagonisms.

In *Capital*, Marx contends repeatedly that only labor can produce more value than it is worth. Other commodities trade at, more or less, the prescribed market price existing and therefore merely pass on their value when turned into finished commodities. That is, wood only increases in value when a worker expends labor upon it and turns it into a desk. Profits come out of the surplus-value workers produce beyond what they are paid. Even when economists ridicule this idea, the labor theory of value is important—as much as a political statement in favor of more social equality as an economic analysis.

The Working Day

Marx starts with the idea that labor-power is bought and sold at its value, which "like that of all other commodities, is determined by the working-time necessary to its production. If the production of the average daily means of subsistence of the laborer takes up six hours, he must work, on the average, six hours every day, to produce his daily labor-power, or to reproduce the value received as the result of its sale. The necessary part of his working-day amounts to six hours …" The capitalist would hardly prosper if he paid the worker the value of his six hours of work. So, by extending the working day past the hours needed for the worker to reproduce his daily labor-power, the capitalist has his employee create value above this minimum, or a surplus-value. It is out of this surplus-value that the capitalist will pay his mortgage, fund his advertising budget, and, of course, get his profits.

So, if the cost of workers today is paid for within four hours, but they have to work eight hours, then there are four hours of surplus-value in the workday for the capitalist to expropriate. Of course, the existence of even huge amounts of surplus-value is no guarantee of profits since the capitalist is competing in an uncertain and hostile marketplace. The political result of this is that working people will have a historical tendency to fight for shorter hours, a demand violently opposed by most employers. Unlike the slave system, the capitalist does not own the worker, who may quit at any time. However, the workers must sell their labor-power in order to survive. So while they are not slaves, they are what might be termed "wage-slaves." That is, they must sell their time to the industrialists for wages in order to survive. Because of the unequal balance of power between the two groups, the capitalist can exploit labor in order to make profits. The workers may be free to labor where they want but ultimately they must sell their labor and their time to an employer.

Historical Critique of Industrialism

Along with his development of economic theory, Karl Marx gives a historical study of the rise of industrial capitalism. He argues that capitalism grew out of the economic structure of feudal society and that the capitalist era dates from at least the sixteenth century. The basis of this process is the expropriation of the agricultural producer, which is the peasant, from the soil. In England, serfdom had all but disappeared by the end of the fourteenth century leaving the vast majority of people as free peasant proprietors. In the late fifteenth and early six-teenth centuries, the balance of class relations changed drastically. The great feudal lords hurled bands of feudal retainers onto the labor market and then drove the peasants off the land, while usurping the common lands. With wool prices rising, it became far more profitable to raise sheep than allow peasant cultivation. Thus it was that Sir Thomas More once remarked, England had be-come a land where sheep devour men. Marx cites contemporary observers who noted, "townes [*sic*] pulled downe [*sic*] for sheepe-walks."

The forcible expropriation of the common people gained a new and terrible impulse from the Reformation under Henry VIII and Elizabeth I. When Henry VIII seized the land of the Catholic Church in England, he was confiscating a great part of England's real estate. Monasteries, convents, and other Roman Catholic Church-run institutions were closed, and the residents thrown into the working class. Church lands were given to favorites and sold cheaply to specu-lators "who drove out, *en masse*, the hereditary subtenants and threw their holdings into one," Marx commented, "The legally guaranteed property of the poorer folk in a part of the church's tithes was tacitly confiscated." Through the last decade of the seventeenth century the yeoman, independent peasants, were more noted than capitalist farmers. Yet, by around 1750, the yeomanry had disappeared. By the last decade of the eighteenth century, the common land of the agricultural worker was no more. This would set the stage for an urban-based capitalism, Marx notes, quoting a long forgotten authority, Dr. Price, "Towns and manufactures will increase, because more will be driven to them in quest of places and employment. This is the way in which the engrossing of farms naturally operates."

Marx estimates that as late as the period of 1801–1831, 3,511,770 acres of common land were stolen from the peasant population. Marx cites the example of the Duchess of Sutherland who decided to "clear" her land of the peasants so that it could be made into a sheep run. As he tells the story, from 1814 till 1820 "15,000 inhabitants, about 3,000 families, were systematically hunted and rooted out. All their villages were destroyed and burned, all their fields turned into pasturage. British soldiers enforced this eviction, and came to blows with the inhabitants. One old woman was burnt to death in the flames of the hut, which she refused to leave." The result was that the Duchess had appropriated to herself 794,000 acres of land that had as long as anyone could remember, belonged to the common people.

Marx discusses the development of the industrial capitalist, who did not develop as gradually as the agricultural capitalist. Preexisting feudal laws and guild regulations had blocked the investment of capital in large-scale industry. The dissolution of the old feudal system reduced some of these barriers, but events conspired to accelerate industrialization even further. Marx comments, the "discovery of gold and silver in America, the extirpation, enslavement and entombment in mines of the aboriginal population, the beginning of the conquest and looting of the East Indies, the turning of Africa into a warren for the commercial hunting of black skins, signal the rosy dawn of the era of capitalist accumulation." In other words, Marx argues that the tremendous wealth looted from overseas, along with the obscenely high profits of the slave trade, combined with internal accumulation of wealth to create an economic basis for the genesis of the Industrial Revolution in England. Whether it was paying cash for every Indian scalp in Puritan New England, the trans-Atlantic slave trade, or selling opium to the Chinese at a vast profit and without regard to the social consequences for China, the capitalist was letting no "old prejudices" stand in the way of progress.

Economic progress was something Marx fervently believed in. At the same time, he was both appalled and shocked as his research revealed to him that this progress, which he hoped would one day free humanity, was based on massive destruction. As he put it in Chapter 31 of *Capital*: "The treasures captured outside Europe by undisguised looting, enslavement and murder floated back to the mother-country and were there turned into capital." Yet, this wealth did little for European commoners as indicated by the great wealth of Holland. By 1648, "the people of Holland were more overworked, poorer and more brutally oppressed than those of all the rest of Europe put together." So, Marx contended that the exploitation of the overseas world created great amounts of capital that could fund an Industrial Revolution, but this wealth often made the life of the masses worse, at least in the short run. The textile industry, in Marx's words, "introduced child-slavery in England," while it accelerated the exploitation of African slaves in the cotton fields of the United States. Still, for all his attacks on the industrial system based on capital, which entered the world "dripping from head to foot, from every pore, with blood and dirt," Marx thought that the resulting industrial system could be tamed to serve the social good.

People Confront the Machines

Although Marx and Engels had argued as early as the *Communist Manifesto* that struggles between classes were a feature of societies since before the Roman Empire, the Industrial Revolution provided a unique twist. While before members of an oppressed class were in conflict only with the dominant class, the new industrial working class was also in conflict with machines. As Marx put it, "only since the introduction of machinery has the workmen fought against the instrument of labor itself." In the seventeenth century, much of Western Europe saw revolts and protests against the ribbon-loom. Invented in Germany, this machine could weave numerous pieces of ribbon at the same time. In the Netherlands, in 1629, riots by weavers caused the Leyden Town Council to outlaw the ribbon-loom. Later, it was forbidden throughout Germany by an imperial edict of February 19, 1685.

This seemingly simple piece of equipment was the precursor of the Industrial Revolution that shook Europe in the eighteenth century. When new innovations appeared, they caused unemployment, which in turn led the people out of work to fight against the new method of production. Often, this protest took the form of destroying the new machines, a key tactic of the Luddite movement, which only gave governments a powerful pretext to pass the most reactionary laws. Luddites hoped that they could prevent the loss of their way of life by attacking innovations in technology when the problem was more changes in the economic system. The people displaced by the machines were the descendants of peasants earlier tossed off the land. "The laborers are first driven from the land," notes *Capital*, "then come the sheep." After the sheep replaced peasants on the land, then the new technology replaced craftsmen.

The expansion of the capitalist system, first and foremost in England, resulted in ever-increasing application of new machinery to the process of production. Unlike previous economic systems, the new industrial capitalism pitted people against machines as the "instrument of labor, when it takes the form of a machine, immediately becomes a competitor of the workman himself." Skilled workers, who because they possessed scarce skills had in the past had job security and even a degree of material comfort, now faced machines that made their skills irrelevant. "That portion of the working class, thus by machinery rendered superfluous ... either goes to the wall in the unequal contest of the old handicrafts and manufactures with machinery ... [or] swamps the labor market," thus reducing wage levels through growing competition for dwindling jobs.

Capital detailed the misery visited upon those who worked in fields where new technology was introduced. Discussing the English handloom weavers, Marx noted that many starved as machinery took over cotton manufacturing. Meanwhile, overseas the English capitalists flooded colonial markets, like those in South Asia, with cheap cloth. The result was, as *Capital* quoted the British Governor General in 1834–1835, "the bones of the cotton-weavers are bleaching the plains of India." This was what defenders of industrial capitalism refer to, Marx indignantly noted, as a temporary inconvenience. Yet, *Capital* is not purely hostile to the Industrial Revolution or machinery. Rather, it is a critique of how it was employed. Marx always stressed that by reducing the amount of manual labor necessary for the production of the needs of life, the Industrial Revolution opened up the possibility of a just society of plenty. Before industrialization, there had to be a class doomed to mindless, unpleasant labor. After the Industrial Revolution, *Capital* looks forward to a world where the most unhealthy and mind-numbing toil would be done by machines.

Response to *Das Kapital*

As important as scholars of all political hues have regarded *Capital* in the generations that followed, the initial response was less than earthshaking. When

Das Kapital was published in Hamburg on September 5, 1867, the overwhelming response was silence. Marx complained that liberals and "vulgar economists" were consciously ignoring his work. Both he and Engels desperately attempted to provoke the establishment economists into responding to the challenge *Capital* posed to their theories. Still, the result was silence. Having given so much of his time, energy, and heart to the publishing project, and getting this feeble reaction, Karl Marx was left dispirited.

Then, in a historical irony, Marx received a letter in October 1868 from a completely overlooked corner of Europe. It was from a young economist named Nikolai Frantsevich Danielson. He informed Marx that N.P. Poliakov, a publisher in St. Petersburg, wanted to print a Russian translation of *Capital*. Further, he was also eager to publish the second volume as soon as Marx could get it ready. Given the fierce censorship that existed in Tsarist Russia, it is strange that *Capital* was not banned. Apparently, the censors who examined the book concluded it was most likely subversive, but too complicated to have any political impact. Thus, Marx's major work was first to become better known in remote, largely agrarian Russia than in the industrial nations he considered his true audience. Another attempt at drawing attention to his work would take place closer to home.

Karl Marx had become a fan of Charles Darwin and his work on the theory of evolution. As he explained in a letter to Ferdinand Lassalle written on January 16, 1861, "very significant is Darwin's book and suits me as a natural history basis for the historical class struggle." So impressed with Charles Darwin was Marx that he sent him a copy of *Capital* in 1872. In a polite response, the natural scientist wrote,

> I thank you for the honor which you have done me by sending me your great work on Capital; and I heartily wish I was more worthy to receive it, by understanding more of the deep and important subject of political economy. Though our studies have been so different, I believe that we both earnestly desire the extension of knowledge, and that this in the long run is sure to add to the happiness of Mankind.

He signed off as "I remain, dear sir, Yours faithfully, Charles Darwin." Later, when Marx asked Darwin if he could dedicate volume two of *Capital* to him, the great scientist declined, saying he did not want to offend religious members of his own family.

When a French translation came out in November 1875, a press run of 10,000 sold out rapidly. In his postscript to the second German edition in 1873, Marx attempted to explain poor sales in Germany by pointing to that nation being less developed than England or France. After the author's death, thanks to the tireless work of Engels, sales of the third edition of *Capital* slowly grew in Germany. This later German edition sold a respectable several hundred copies a year during the 1880s and 1890s. Later, *Capital* would become even more widely acknowledged, although it was more often mentioned than actually read by socialist and labor leaders.

While the first German edition appeared in 1867, it would be twenty years before a complete English language version would see the light of day. Until the English edition finally appeared, Anglo-Saxons who wished to study it had to struggle with the German, French, or Russian editions. In one case, English radical Peter Fox received a copy of the German edition. He is said to have remarked that he felt rather like a man who had been given an elephant and had no idea what to do with it. As Marx died in 1883, the burden of overseeing this translation fell on Engels. In a letter to Laura Lafargue, Marx's daughter, dated April 28, 1886, he complained, "The English translation of *Capital* is awful work ... Then I revise and enter suggestions in pencil. Then it goes back to them. Then conference for settlement of doubtful points. Then I have to go through the whole again ..."

All the same, even in the United States, Samuel Gompers, leader of the relatively conservative American Federation of Labor (AFL) read it. Eugene V. Debs, leader of the American Railroad workers and later Socialist candidate for president, got through *Capital* while serving time in a Woodstock, Illinois, jail for leading a strike. In fact, *Capital* was to sell better in the United States than in England—partly because, in 1890, a clever New York publisher promoted it to bank officials as a book explaining how to accumulate capital. This ironically caused a press run of 5,000 to sell out—albeit not so much to workers but largely to the type of people Marx was attacking. Slowly, editions of *Capital* appeared in various other languages, with translations in Spanish, Italian, Polish, Danish, and Dutch by the mid-1890s. Today, in the twenty-first century, there is not a major language in which a translation of *Capital* cannot be found.

Importance of Marx's Capital

Even critics of Marx's economic theory often give him credit for pointing out aspects of capitalism that orthodox economists have overlooked or downplayed. For one thing, capitalist economists have often given the market almost godlike powers. As the old joke goes, how many economists does it take to change a light bulb? Well, if the bulb needs changing the market will do it. Marx, by contrast, always looked beyond market relations to see human relations. He emphasized that there was no inherent harmony between capitalists and workers because the former wanted to increase profits and thus lower wages and other costs of production, while the latter rather obviously wanted better wages and working conditions. This realization has been granted by even economists who believe Marx's labor theory of value otherwise discredited.

Marx attacks the idea that the capitalist market is self-regulating and will correct itself most rapidly if it is left unregulated. Interestingly enough, this idea was widely accepted in the United States in the 1920s. Pointing to the history of a boom-and-bust trade cycle in capitalism, Marx points to this as an inherent part of the system. With the onset of the Great Depression of 1929, many were forced to, at least partially, grant Marx's point about the boom-and-bust nature of unregulated capitalism. To many others, *Capital*'s account of the exploitative relation of boss to the worker is strongly compelling.

One of the great strengths of *Capital* is that Marx goes beyond blaming evil people for society's problems. Instead, he attempts to analyze the ways in which exploitation is inherent within the capitalist system regardless of an individual bourgeois's personality. Marx points out that if any one businessman refuses, let us say for humanitarian reasons, to be as ruthless as his competitors he will simply be pushed out of the mainstream of the economy. After all, the market rewards the "most efficient" companies not the nicest companies. To survive in a competitive marketplace, an employer had best not worry about mercy but instead of his/her bottom line. The only way that this race to bottom can be slowed or maybe stopped is by the collective action of employees uniting to push back capitalist demands for more work, in worse conditions at lower real wages. This means political action such as the formation of independent trade unions and political parties that can fight on behalf of the common people.

Moreover, Marx never insisted that the condition of the masses had to become ever worse in terms of living conditions and real wages. Rather, he contended that their poverty would be *relatively* worse as they received a small portion of society's wealth, even if their standard of living rose. At first, this seems rather strange. If one has more of the good things of life then surely one is better off? Karl Marx, explained as early as *Wage Labor and Capital*, that it is not just the absolute amount of wealth an individual possesses, it is what it represents within the society one lives in. As Marx explains, "A house may be large or small; as long as the surrounding houses are equally small it satisfies all social demands for a dwelling. But let a palace arise beside the little house, and it shrinks from a little house to a hut." This all happens because, as Marx saw it, our desires beyond the most basic like hunger are of a social nature. In the twenty-first century, a rather large flat screen television may be considered a "necessity" in some societies.

Capital provides a very lively picture of how capitalism works, not so much merely in the nineteenth century but rather in the twenty-first century. The claims it made for what is now called globalization must have seemed rather far fetched to people living in the era of horse-drawn carriages but now are the commonplace utterances of the business press such as the *Financial Times*. As Francis Wheen, one of Marx's more recent biographers noted, "Far from being buried under the rubble of the Berlin Wall, Marx may only now be emerging in his true significance. He could yet become the most influential thinker of the twenty-first century." In fact, during the financial crisis in 2009, the business section of the *Atlantic Times* editorialized that as "the current crisis again demonstrates, unchecked speculation ends in disaster. Swooning stock markets cause a credit crunch, this then results in recession. An old book—volume 3 of *Das Kapital*—tells all about it."

6

"All I Know Is I'm Not a Marxist": Marx's Last Years

Introduction

At the conclusion of the Hague Congress, Karl Marx traveled to Amsterdam and addressed a meeting of workers on September 8, 1872. This and other details of his movements were carefully monitored by a host of police spies. If these agents hoped to discover some dastardly plot against Western civilization, they were surely disappointed. The German-born activist continued to argue for his view of a new type of industrial society that would be achieved by openly organized and politicized class struggles. People who met Marx in person, even police spies and aristocrats, were always surprised at what a nice "gentleman" he was. There was much truth in what Engels said in his funeral oration, when he had claimed that Marx "may have had many opponents, he had hardly one personal enemy." The stories that otherwise hostile observers told about the German refugee would appear to confirm Engels' contention.

Marx, the "Nice Gentleman"

A few examples of this unanticipated reaction may well give us something about Marx as a person rather than a political legend. Returning from a visit to Hamburg in 1867, where he had turned over the first volume of *Capital* to the publisher Otto Meissner, he decided to stop in Hanover to visit his old friend Ludwig Kugelmann. While there, a strange story unfolded. Marx was approached by a man named Warnebold, who claimed that the German chancellor Otto von Bismarck wished to win him to his service. Even now, it is hard to know if this was a serious offer on Bismarck's part, but Marx never considered it for a moment.

Then on his journey back to London, one of history's little ironies was to throw him into contact with, not Bismarck, but his niece. On the boat back to England, a young German woman asked Marx if he knew any details about railroad connections once they reached London. It became clear that she would have to wait several hours before her train, and the German radical gallantly helped her pass time by taking her for a walk in Hyde Park. She turned out to be Elizabeth von Puttkamer, who had just come from staying some weeks with her uncle in Berlin, Otto von Bismarck. When she found out who the kindly old gentleman was, she was surprised, in the words of a later letter by Marx describing the incident "that she had fallen into red hands." At the same, she enjoyed Marx's company so much that she wrote a letter of "heartfelt thanks" for all the trouble he had gone to for her. Even her more politically conscious parents felt the necessity to write and tell the author of *Capital* that they were glad to find out that a young woman could still meet "good men" on a journey.

Later in 1879, the eldest daughter of British Queen Victoria, Crown Princess Victoria asked a politician (who had the rather complicated name of Sir Mountstuart Elphinstone Grant Duff) about this Dr. Marx she was hearing so much about. Sir Mountstuart, eager to please not only his Queen but also her daughter, the wife of future German Kaiser Frederick III, invited Karl Marx for lunch. The member of Parliament reported spending three hours with Dr. Marx and since the latter enjoyed good food and drink—there is little doubt that the aging radical had an enjoyable afternoon.

Sir Mountstuart Duff was surprised to find a "well-informed, nay; learned man." Rather unexpectedly, Dr. Marx turned out to be more "pleasant than not, by no means [giving the impression] of a gentleman who is in the habit of eating babies in their cradles—which is I daresay the view which the Police takes of him." Nor was there any of the "Marat tone" in the German intellectual's conversation. Duff goes so far as to note approvingly that when the subject arose of "the horrible things that have been connected with the International he [Marx] spoke as any respectable man would have."

During the luncheon, Marx predicted an ever-increasing arms race that would, sooner or later, lead to war among the great powers. This war would unleash, Marx argued, misery and popular revolution. Sir Mountstuart dismissed this as a possibility and thus dismissed any danger arising from Marx's ideas, which were "too dreamy to be dangerous except just in so far as the situation with its mad expenditure on armaments is obviously and undoubtedly dangerous." Ultimately, World War I would seem to prove Marx rather Duff the winner of that particular tabletop debate.

Even a reporter from the famously anti-labor *Chicago Tribune* who visited the Marx home around Christmas in 1878 was forced to admit: "Persistently during all these years, he has advocated his views with an earnestness which undoubtedly springs from his firm belief in them, and however much we may depreciate their propagation, we cannot but respect to a certain extent the self-denial of the now venerable exile." The Midwestern journalist was forced to contradict the stories of Marx, growing rich off the back of unsuspecting workers and supporters. "His convictions have caused him trouble from the beginning," the *Chicago Tribune* wrote. "Judging from the appearance of his home, they certainly have not brought him affluence."

Marx's health in these years was little better than that of the First International. Yet, it would be an exaggeration to see Marx's last years as only some sort of slow decline and death. Like most people of all ages, the coauthor of the *Communist Manifesto* had good days and bad days. Some of his friends thought that a complete restoration of his health might have been possible if Marx would lessen his work load, something he would not hear of.

In fact, his habits were not the best when considered from the standpoint of health. He stayed up working late into the night yet he always woke up early the next morning. He drank impressive quantities of strong black coffee while often forgetting to eat and generally possessing a poor appetite. According to Franz Mehring, one of his early leftist biographers, Marx "was accustomed to say jokingly that his *Capital* would not bring him in sufficient to pay for the cigars he had smoked whilst writing it [there is little doubt] his passion for smoking certainly did his health no good." This tobacco addiction was to continue despite the fact that his doctor prohibited his smoking on numerous occasions.

Plagued by illness that seemed to be worsening in 1874, Marx ventured to Carlsbad, Germany, to recoup his energy. While he felt the "cure" at this famous spa did him a world of good, it most likely did little to eliminate his underlying health problems. Back in London, his living conditions took a turn for the better when, in 1875, the Marx family moved to a new and nicer house, thanks to the financial generosity of Engels.

The new dwelling quickly became a hub of activity as radicals, both notable and obscure, made frequent appearances. Despite ill health and the continued press of these visitors, the aging revolutionary plugged away on further volumes of *Capital*. Not only expanded manuscripts for future publication, but also the editing and correction of the existing volume in new languages made claims on Marx's time.

European Socialism Grows

As he continued his work on *Capital*, Marx watched with both excitement and apprehension at the growth of socialist parties throughout Europe. Preexisting radical and republican hatreds of the rich and the "plutocracy" intensified after the Paris Commune in 1871. The experience of industrialization finally convinced many, particularly manual workers who did physical labor with their hands, of the injustice of the status quo. As workers living in slums like Berlin's Wedding or West Ham in London felt increasingly distant from the world of the bourgeoisie, proletarians viewed political issues such as the fight for extension of voting rights from an increasingly socialist perspective.

As noted before, the focus of these movements tended to be more national than international. There was certain logic to this: As governments were national in scope, any effort to win reforms would seem best handled on the national stage. In a way, the very organization of European nation-states helped push the working class in each country toward the formation of national, class-based parties.

Choosing different names depending on the local traditions and the politics of the moment, most of these parties called themselves *labor, socialist,* or *social democratic*, as these terms were interchangeable in the nineteenth century. Pablo Iglesias, who was to be the first socialist in the Spanish parliament, helped form the Spanish Socialist Workers Party in 1879. The same year saw a Danish socialist party established. Three years later, France's *Parti* Ouvrier [Workers Party] was organized by Jules Guesde and five years thereafter a Norwegian Labor Party began. In 1888, socialist political parties were established in both Switzerland and the Austro-Hungarian Empire followed a year later by a new party in Sweden. The most powerful of these parties was to be the Social Democratic Party of Germany (SPD), formed in 1875 by the combination of two hitherto hostile groupings: Lassalleans, who attempted to collaborate with Bismarck's government, and the Marxist-oriented Eisenachers, who claimed to be followers of Marx.

Despite a series of repressive antisocialist laws enacted by the German Reichstag in 1878, the Social Democrats, under the leadership of August Bebel and Wilhelm Liebknecht became an "empire within an empire." The election data would support this proposition. Starting with less than 125,000 votes in 1871, the German Social Democrats would gather more than 500,000 votes in 1884. Six years later, more than one million German men (women could not as yet vote) cast their ballots for the SPD.

More than just an electoral machine, the Germans possessed what might be fairly called a press empire. By the end of the nineteenth century, they had seventy-five papers, of which over half were published daily. Besides their theoretical journal *Die Neue Zeit* (the New Age), which advanced Marxist theory, there were a surprising number of nonpolitical publications affiliated with the party. Among the latter were various special-interest publications, many with a circulation more than 100,000. Thus, a radical intellectual could spend the evening perusing the pages of *Die Neue Zeit,* while the less theoretically oriented worker could spend their free time with *Der Arbeiter Radfahrer* (Worker Cyclist) or the *Arbeiter Turnzeitung* (Worker Gymnastic Newspaper). Even socialist innkeepers and stenographers had their own publications.

The party created an entire alternative world for its supporters. If a worker wanted to borrow a novel, there were worker libraries. Those who wished to sing could join "red" singing societies. For those who enjoyed beer or wine, there were frequent meetings and dinners in beer halls and cafes, while those with a drinking problem could join the German Workers Temperance Federation, a sort of socialist Alcoholics Anonymous. All these activities created a sense of belonging and group solidarity among socialist workers who otherwise might have been isolated or demoralized.

While other socialist parties could not match the level of electoral success enjoyed by the German party, they were, nonetheless, steadily growing in popularity among the masses. Each party was fashioned within the traditions of its country and heavily influenced by the leaders who gave it direction. The French or Spanish parties might lack the iron discipline and overt Marxist rhetoric of the Austrian or German parties. Even the most "orthodox" Marxist parties would, in reality, develop their own manner of functioning in response to the conditions existing at any given time.

All these parties agreed that socialists should focus on political activity to promote the cause of labor. This emphasis on politics defined socialists as distinct from those like the anarchists who rejected politics or people who preached self-help like the cooperative movement or the various and assorted Christian dominations that promoted faith in the hereafter. European socialists believed that, as capitalism continued to develop, only two social classes within society would matter: a smaller, if powerful, bourgeoisie and a growing working class, which would make up the vast majority of the population. What had been a major class, the peasantry, was viewed as historically doomed. The mechanization of agriculture, socialists believed, would force the peasants from the land, as they were no longer needed in any significant number.

After the dark years following the destruction of the Paris Commune, Marx was naturally excited that the left was growing once again. At the same time, he often despaired at what he saw as the fuzzy politics of these new parties. While his reputation was now such that most in these rising socialist parties claimed inspiration from his work, their interpretation often drove Marx (and Engels) to the heights of frustration. Reflecting on this period in a letter from 1890, Engels commented that, by the late 1870s, Marx had become fond of saying privately: "all I know is that I am not a Marxist."

It was particularly painful for the London exile to watch helplessly as his German supporters united with rival socialists of dubious political pedigree. Karl Marx had always worried about the ideological clarity of Wilhelm Liebknecht and August Bebel, leaders of the German socialists claiming to follow Marx. The Liebknecht/Bebel group fused with the socialists known as Lassalleans to form one united German socialist party. Instead of being happy at the creation of a stronger workers party in his native land, Marx was beside himself.

After reading a draft of the new program to be adopted in the German city of Gotha, Marx was furious at his German followers.

While recognizing that "every step of real movement is more important than a dozen programs," Marx still could not understand why his supposed followers had agreed to a public program so alien to his views. In a letter to Wilhelm Bracke written in May 1875, he asks why further common action could not have been attempted before formal unification. Seemingly more concerned with political purity than practical politics, Marx was convinced the new program would only confuse German socialists. His detailed objections to this party platform would be published after his death as *Critique of the Gotha Program*, the main point of which is concisely summed up in the letter mentioned above where Marx states flatly "the program is no good."

European Socialists React to Marx's Criticism

For their part, the German socialists paid no real attention to these criticisms. To them, the unification represented progress, and they cared little if they had to make a few tactical concessions to achieve their goal. This conflict between Marx's more insistent emphasis on theory and socialist leaders' desire for quick results were to be a continuing source of tension between Karl Marx and those who claimed to follow him. Their disregard for ideology was not entirely surprising when one considers that the Industrial Revolution was creating an ever larger and potentially powerful working class in Western Europe. The times appeared to call for action rather than theoretical deliberations.

As once small groups mushroomed into massive parties, this drive for action rather than reflection must have been overpowering. European socialist parties became conflicted between a long-term program (owing much to Marx and Engels) including radical things like popular control of industry and a short-term program of immediate moderate demands that often including things like more public parks. Any given left party leadership believed that socialism was the only ultimate solution, but while the final conflict was emerging, mundane issues like sewers and taxes had to be addressed. Where socialists were able to participate in elections, there was always pressure to appeal to nonsocialist, but alienated, voters by raising popular reformist demands.

Marx and Engels, who thought that their writings would lead to revolutionary political action, found their writings used to justify inaction by party leaders. If the Industrial Revolution made socialism inevitable, why not concentrate on reforms that would make life a little easier while the workers waited for the better world to come? Marx actually argued industrialization made socialism possible but not inevitable. This was a sophisticated nuance that many missed. On May 12, 1878, matters took a clear turn for the worse when an attempt was made to assassinate the ruler of the German Empire. Although the crime was in no way supported by the socialists, the government of Chancellor Otto von Bismarck made them the scapegoat. As Marx had argued in his controversies with the anarchists, this act of violence did not rouse the masses but rather gave the authorities an excuse to persecute the movement. The growing socialist community in Germany soon found its party outlawed, the labor press banned, leaders exiled or jailed. Despite the new obstacles, the movement continued and even prospered.

Otto von Bismarck was not like Hitler and the later Nazis, who murdered their leftist opponents. In fact, under Bismarck's repressive laws, the socialists could still run as independents for the German parliament, or Reichstag. Whether by design (some say Bismarck knew the carrot was as important as the stick) or chance, the ability to continue election campaigns strengthened moderates and non-Marxists within German socialism. Since it was necessary to tailor election campaigns to the restrictions imposed by the antisocialist laws, the cautious tended to become prominent while the radical suffered exile or jail. Still, new members and voters flocked to the outlawed party. Watching from London, Marx was powerless to do more than write impassioned letters, which were mainly ignored. While the antisocialist laws were in effect, German socialists could always shrug their shoulders and say they agreed with Marx but were powerless under the circumstances.

In France, Marx and Engels had a direct hand in drafting the *Program of the Parti Ouvier* (Workers Party), which they wrote with the help of left-winger Jules Guesde and Marx's son-in-law Paul Lafargue. Nonetheless, conflicts quickly arose between Karl Marx and his French friends. While the ailing German theorist felt that minimum demands were a practical part of the program for organizing people around achievable goals, Guede viewed them with contempt as merely "bait to lure workers from radicalism." Marx was furious that Guede did not value the importance of winning reforms in building the socialist movement. Perhaps even more upsetting was that Marx's son-in-law Lafargue sided with Guede. All of this did nothing to diminish the German exile from venting to Engels his frustration with the French. It may not have helped that his two eldest daughters married Frenchmen who often irritated Marx one way or another. At one point in the 1870s, his youngest daughter Eleanor, appeared headed toward marriage with Prosper Lissagary, an exile from the Paris Commune. Karl Marx, the German father, won out over Marx, the internationalist, and Eleanor was advised to find a more suitable husband. By the time he relented, Eleanor had grown tired of Lissagary, the former Communard and they never married. Sadly she did not find someone better, taking up with the Englishman Edward Aveling, who turned out to be an emotionally abusive womanizer.

The aging exile was not singling out the French for abuse. He found almost all the socialist movements and leaders lacking in either talent or principle and occasionally both. In part, this was the frustration of a once active leader now cut off from continental Europe by his English exile. The antisocialist laws of Bismarck made trips to Germany dangerous, and his failing health caused all travel to be burdensome and potentially dangerous. Forced onto the sidelines, Marx could only write letters to European socialist leaders. Often, these letters were warmly welcomed as a great help to the movement and then disregarded.

Sometimes Marx himself was even ignored. Yet, even when his advice was unwelcome, he was not forgotten. Maybe few could make it all the way through a reading of *Capital*, and fewer still could really understand all its nuances, but Marx was seen as something like the nineteenth-century equivalent of a rock star by radicals and workers.

Frustrations and Old Age

It was ironic that Marx, the perfectionist, so often ranted against the movement his theories had helped to shape and inspire. The working-class socialist movement, which routinely invoked the names of Marx and Engels, may have been flawed, but was real and growing rapidly. When fuming over misinterpretations of his writings, Marx forgot the adage that an author loses control of their work the second it is published. Maybe as he aged, Dr. Marx took on too much of the persona of a German philosophy professor, the occupation he originally set for himself. After all, much of his theoretical hairsplitting made perfect sense to other philosophers but probably not as much to an average factory worker. The great success of Marx was in his central premise that argued industrialism should be embraced, and then redirected, but not rejected. In the recounting of tactical disputes between Marx and his followers, it is easy to overlook the fact that almost all European socialists agreed with his take on the Industrial Revolution. This was, in and of itself, a monumental accomplishment.

Those who opposed industrialism in the name of socialism (or the people) were fewer, weaker, and more isolated because of Marx's work. When Marx first entered the political fray as a young man, utopian socialist schemes were popular, anarchism was a rising movement, and various other anti-industrial ideologies were attached to the labor movement. By the early 1880s, the final years of Marx's life, the anti-industrial movements were all in retreat, if not reduced to meaningless small cults. The future would hold other departures from Marx, but given the diversity of historical developments that is hardly surprising.

What is ultimately compelling is that Marx was able to overcome the division between the pro-industrialists who worshiped at the feet of Capital and the anti-industrialists who feared every technological advance. Instead, he put forth the idea of the Industrial Revolution as a liberating development, but only if it was tamed by popular mass democracy to serve the many instead of the few. In promoting this view, Marx set a standard that was largely adopted by European socialist parties. Even the moderates felt they had to acknowledge Marx, and many left-wing politicians in Europe still do. If Marx came back to life, he would doubtless be horrified by many things and saddened by others. However, he could still be proud to hear that parties who claimed his legacy are responsible for many social reforms in Western Europe, such as strong unions, national healthcare, universal education, and wider democratic rights.

The Last of Marx

By the 1880s, Karl Marx was increasingly a spent force physically. Fortunately for him, ever-loyal Engels was still healthy (he was to live until 1895) and took over much of the theoretical work. The clear beginning of the end for Marx was when his beloved and faithful wife, Jenny, died on December 12, 1881. Although he lingered for a few years and even had an occasional spark of the old political fighter, Engels was right when, at the time, he stated, "Marx has died, too." Emotionally shattered and in failing health, Marx spent most of 1882 traveling.

He visited Algeria, France, and Switzerland and visited his two eldest daughters, Jenny and Laura. He even visited Monte Carlo and its famous casino, where he apparently watched the wife of a Russian official lose 6,000 francs. Marx found people floating through the entire Monte Carlo milieu ridiculous to the extreme. Writing his youngest daughter, Marx exclaimed, "What childishness this gambling table is compared to the Stock Exchange!" One would think that a dying man of at best modest means would find the sight of all that money being tossed about depressing; instead the frantic money losing seems to have given Marx a good laugh.

Although Karl Marx was dying, he hid the worst of the doctor's news from his family and continued to retain his intellectual curiosity and ability to become excited. Arriving in Paris in June 1882, he was met by son-in-law Paul Lafargue. Instead of the sick old man Lafargue had expected, Marx was animated with stories of his encounters with Africans and Arabs. The excited Marx could apparently not hold his tongue and proceeded to treat Paul to a monologue of all the peoples he had met and impressions he had formed. This continued for what appeared to be an eternity to Marx's patient French son-in-law when suddenly the aged revolutionary demanded to know why Lafargue had given him no news of the family. With a tone of amused exacerbation, the Frenchman exclaimed "Good heavens, you didn't give me a chance to get a word in!"

Throughout his last months, he was comforted by his daughters (particularly Eleanor), and as always by the intellectual bond with Engels. After eldest daughter Jenny Longuet died of cancer in Paris on January 11, 1883, little was left of Karl Marx the man, if Marx the fighter still at times found the energy to rage in letters. Before his end, he gave his daughter Eleanor the task of preparing his manuscripts for publication and supervising an English publication of *Capital*. (Sadly, she was betrayed by her lover Edward Aveling who secretly married another woman, Eleanor took her own life in 1898.)

Two months later, Engels would report "On the 14th of March, at a quarter to three in the afternoon, the greatest living thinker ceased to think. He had been left alone for scarcely two minutes, and when we came back, we found him in his armchair peacefully gone to sleep, but forever." Apparently, this is the way Marx wanted to go out of the land of the living. He may have even resisted medical treatment. As Engels commented in a letter written shortly afterward, medical "skill might have been able to give him a few more years of vegetative existence, the life of a helpless being, dying to the triumph of the doctor's art, not suddenly, but inch by inch. But our Marx could never have born [such a life that] would have been a thousand times more bitter than the gentle death which overtook him."

Tributes were paid to the dead revolutionary from all parts of the industrialized world. For the Germans, socialist leader Wilhelm Liebknecht eulogized that Marx had a great heart as well as a great mind and said that, although a heavy blow the "deceased is not dead. He lives in the *heart*; he lives in the *head* of the proletariat." Naturally, there were similar sentiments expressed in France, Russia, and other European countries.

Even in the United States, which had served as the deathbed of the First International, Marx's departure caused a minor stir. The *New York Times* on March 16, 1883, reported that various unions, labor, and radical groups gathered at New York's Cooper Union, where Abraham Lincoln had once given a famous address, to pay their compliments to the expired German revolutionary. At the meeting, speakers reflected on Marx's importance, noting that people of labor and science had both "lost an able and devoted champion." Further, it was put forth that Marx gave his life "to the service of mankind. His labor, writings, and all his energies were given to the cause of human advancement and to the liberation of all downtrodden people. And now it is the duty of all true lovers of liberty to honor the name of Karl Marx."

7

The Meaning of Marx

Introduction

In his *Age of Capital*, renowned historian Eric Hobsbawm credits Karl Marx with being the most important leader of the "forces of democracy." At first, this statement may seem paradoxical, as Marx is as often portrayed as an enemy of democracy. While Marx thought that existing institutions of government (the state) had to be torn down, it would be a mistake to conclude that he was hostile to democracy itself. In fact, his view was quite the opposite. He held that all existing governments had been little more than the expression of one or another ruling class that used the state apparatus to maintain control over the common people. To end this dictatorship of an elite, Marx felt a truly radical democracy was needed that would allow the popular will to address the people's needs. It is a testament to the undemocratic nature of modern culture that the term "populist" is so often used as a term of abuse.

It was never true, as hostile critics have charged that Marx opposed elections. At one point, he thought free elections in the United States would allow a socialist transformation without violence. Rather, he was in opposition to elections designed to ensure the maintenance of the status quo. For Marx, a life-long enemy of monarchy, dictatorship, and all antidemocratic institutions, the solution to society's woes was more democracy not less. In his day, he spoke out against the property restriction that limited the vote to the well-off, and he supported women's suffrage. In his writings about the United States, he repeatedly and forcefully argued that white workers must accept black workers as equals. At the risk of redundancy, a summary of some of Marx's main contributions remains in order.

Internationalism, Solidarity, and Opposition to Imperialism

Marx realized that the revolutionary struggle to transform society had to be international in scope if it were to succeed. Long before it was fashionable to speak of the world as a "global community," Marx argued that the spread of industrialization would cause ever-deeper interconnections between all peoples of the world. Marx believed that establishing a social republic in only one nation or region alone was not practical or sustainable. The outside capitalist powers would eventually overwhelm such a government. While Marx could have only dreamed of the role of new technology in the twenty-first century, he saw as early as the 1840s the progress of industrial capitalism constantly reinventing itself at always higher levels of technology.

As the bourgeoisie became more international and cosmopolitan, it became more detached from both nation-states and ethnicity. Marx noted that the bourgeoisie increasingly were transformed into a transnational class. By 2011, an autoworker in the United States was just as likely to be employed by an East Asian or European corporation as by a North American-based company. Many Fords are built in Mexico, while Hondas and Toyotas are manufactured in Ohio and Mississippi, respectively. Marx contended that to struggle against an international capitalist class, the working class would necessarily have to become more globally minded if it hoped to win reforms. For all its notable failings, the First International was an important, if largely symbolic, attempt to promote working-class internationalism.

Given his strong emphasis on the importance of universal voting rights and popular movements, Marx should be considered a champion of democratic values and not a spiritual godfather of authoritarian regimes. Karl Marx was above all a proponent of freedom; not, of course, freedom for a minority to exploit and oppress the majority, but freedom for all to have a decent standard of living. In any conflict between property rights and human rights, Marx was firmly on the side of the latter. In his writings on Ireland, for example, he acknowledged the legal "right" of English landlords to export food while the Irish poor died like flies. However, this was a property right he found incompatible with the human rights of the Irish.

His firm stance in favor of popular democracy was not motivated by the illusion that the working class was morally superior to other classes per se. Despite his fervent belief in democracy, Marx was far from the stereotypical starry-eyed idealist. He knew that people typically looked after their own perceived self-interest. Thus, his writings have little use for those who spout platitudes about the inherent goodness of humankind. Marx had only contempt for those who argued that the rich and powerful would renounce their positions and privileges en masse. Some radicals thought that reason alone would convince the dominant elite to abdicate in favor of the masses. One example was Ferdinand Lassalle, leader of a section of the German labor movement, who worked for an alliance with the "Iron Chancellor" Otto von Bismarck. Lassalle, to whom Marx and Engels referred in their letters as an "uncertain friend," thought he could bring socialism to Germany by making deals with the old *Junker* (feudal) ruling class. It is no surprise that when Marx heard of this proposal he was livid with rage.

Rejection of Racism

As a person who grew up in the nineteenth century, Marx in his more unguarded personal moments was not above using ethnic slurs, but he consciously opposed the idea that humanity was divided into superior and inferior races. Living at a time when racism was widespread, promoted as scientific and respectable, Marx all the same rejected the idea of innate ethnically based traits. Support for, or at least toleration of, slavery was commonplace in Marx's time. A man as renowned as John Locke, sometimes called the British "philosopher of liberty," was a founding owner of the primary British slave trading company.

Although it would have been easy for Marx to surrender to the prejudices of his age, he remained an uncompromising opponent of human slavery. During the Civil War in the United States, he did all he could to rally German immigrants in the United States to the cause of the Union and abolition of slavery. He famously admonished American workers to understand that "labor in a white skin can never be free if labor in a black skin is enslaved." In England, he used the International Working Men's Association to promote support for Lincoln and the North. Meanwhile on a more personal level, he had a warm, if at times politically conflicted, relation with his mixed race son-in-law Paul Lafargue. This may not sound so significant in the twenty-first century but was sadly rare in the nineteenth.

Independent Political Action

Another school of thought held that the power of example could compel the upper class into adopting socialism. These people, tagged "utopian socialists" by Marx, believed that socialist communities should be established to demonstrate the superiority of cooperation over competition. Some, like British industrialist Robert Owen, went beyond theory and actually set up model communities like

New Harmony, Indiana. In response to this idea, particularly as articulated by the French thinker Prodhoun, Marx wrote that this was little more than trying to "build the new society behind the back of the old."

If neither deals with the powers-that-be nor the power of example impressed Marx, what did? For him, the answer was in the democratic activity of the masses themselves. In Marx's words enshrined in the statutes of the International Working Men's Association, "the emancipation of the working class must be the work of the working class itself." One might reasonably ask why. Remember, it was not that Marx thought workers were any more moral, capable, or noble than members of other classes. Rather, he thought the working class had the power to change society in a way that would not only benefit them but would also emancipate all of society. Workers had the power because they supplied the labor-power that made the entire industrial system function. If the workers were to go on strike, everything would come to a halt. He rejected the popular notion that property was the wellspring of all liberty and asked what happens to those with little or no property. Do the latter, Marx thundered, deserve liberty any less than the rich?

Marx reasoned that any small ruling group would keep privilege and power to themselves. On the other hand, with the working class representing an ever-increasing majority of the population, they could achieve their liberation only in conjunction with other members of society. Although numerically small numbers of either feudal lords or later big capitalists could rule without any concern for the masses, the working class comprised a large portion of the population, and could only take care of itself by taking care of others. Granted, the occasional duke or billionaire might find life less pleasurable, but to Marx, this would be a small price to pay to allow the vast mass of humanity to realize its potential. The realm of freedom would be greatly expanded, save for those wishing to exploit, oppress, or enslave. Firmly committed to the idea that means influences ends, Marx saw the worker's revolution must necessarily be democratic, since otherwise socialism and equality could not be achieved. Only with democracy could workers rule themselves and not be ruled by others.

Opposition to Terrorism

Marx's concept of independent action did not include the impulsive turn to individual violence. Michael Bakunin, along with various and sundry anarchists, had pushed for action at any price. They preached "propaganda of the deed" whereby individual actions of terror (such as the assassination of rulers and government officials) would somehow ignite a revolutionary response from the oppressed masses. Given the poverty and a sense of hopelessness among portions of the population, the idea of individual terror found a small but vocal audience.

Marx never wavered from his rejection of this tactic. He saw it not only as morally repugnant but also politically self-defeating. Repeatedly he asserted that terror was the friend of reactionary governments who would use "propaganda of the deed" as a pretext to crack down on the workers movement. Further, dramatic individual acts risked becoming a substitute for the mass democratic activity that Marx advocated.

All the same, it would be a mistake to think Marx's rejection of terror was mainly based on tactical considerations. More fundamentally, he argued that a better world could never arise by destroying the achievements of the past, among which he counted the Industrial Revolution. Marx the historian saw terrorism as an ugly remnant of past ages when power-hungry minorities imposed their will on an unwilling populace. For socialism to come about, the overwhelming majority of the population would have to be convinced of its desirability. This would be the type of system that would build upon and expand on concepts like free speech, elections, and civil liberties. Terrorism, even if based on noble ideas and successful in execution, could only usher in another society ultimately based on violence.

Despite his opposition to the tactics of terrorism, Marx was not a pacifist. He understood the need for force at points in history as his outspoken support for a Northern military victory during the U.S. Civil War indicates. Further, he expected that even the most popular and peaceful revolution would encounter resistance from those who sought to keep their power and privilege much as the Southern slave owners took up arms against the legal U.S. government to maintain their "freedom" to own slaves. In response to resistance by this entrenched minority, workers and other common people would be compelled to use their social power, most notably their ability to withhold their labor through strikes, to enforce the popular will. Unlike his anarchist political rivals, Marx never targeted individuals. It was the capitalist system that was his enemy.

Working-Class Organization

Rather than violence, Marx preached organization. He appreciated the powerlessness of workers as individuals. An individual member of the bourgeoisie might have influence through their ownership of part of the means of production. Still, the failure of even Robert Owen and his considerable wealth to sustain utopian communities illustrates, even the power of an individual with money has its limits. For the working class, it was especially clear that individual action was inadequate to institute real social change. Therefore, Marx was an advocate of the laboring class pooling their talents and resources to build organizations that would be able to articulate, and ultimately implement, their demands. These institutions would fall into two basic categories.

First, those who worked for a living would need to unite in their workplaces and industries to form economic organizations, or what is commonly called unions. These unions would battle the capitalist in the economic sphere to preserve and advance working people's standard of living. By collectively presenting their demands, and if need be withholding their labor, a group of organized workers could achieve far more than if they attempted to fight as individuals. All the same, these struggles at the point of production or distribution were in the long term defensive in nature. What was gained in times of a labor shortage within any given field or occupation would quickly be lost if there was a surplus of unemployed who could replace vocal workers. Additionally, if the government passed anti-labor legislation, the fight of unions would be limited to minor triumphs at best.

Thus, Marx emphasized the need for pro-working class political parties that would defend the rights of the unions and the common people as a whole. These parties should not only struggle against laws that would cripple organizing, but they should also pressure the establishment to make such concessions as universal free education, health and safety regulation, and equal pay for equal work rules. Since every reform won would strengthen the working-class cause, these radical parties had to fight for immediate reforms. Yet, Marx argued that they must at the same time point out the larger structural inequalities inherent in the present system. In other words, the parties needed to remind society that the common people did the work in the factories while the owners lived large off the profits from the workers' production. Ultimately, more than reforms were needed to correct such a basic injustice.

Class Struggle

Marx's method of argument demonstrates his material analysis of the international revolution in production, in contrast to abstract morals and principles. Although capable of great moral outrage, as seen in his writings on American slavery, the plight of the Irish poor, and India's suffering under British colonialism, Marx held that all serious thought must proceed from an open-minded examination of conditions as they are, not as one would wish they were. Karl Marx was never an economic determinist, as often charged, since he consistently acknowledged the role of ideas and collective action in shaping history. However, he always stressed the need to study concrete realities; he believed that a clear understanding of industrial society was more useful than any number of well-intended utopian dreams.

The motor force of history, according to Marx, was the conflict between different socioeconomic groups competing for scarce resources. He believed in the centrality of class struggle in human history, which he expressed clearly in the *Communist Manifesto*. A closer examination of this often-cited (but less frequently read) work illustrates Marx's theory. In Section I, proclaiming that the "history of all hitherto existing societies is the history of class struggles," the authors unveil their contention that conflict and not cooperation drives society. It is important to add that Marx and Engels were referring here only to the written history of state societies, not the history of earlier, and more egalitarian, forms of human organization.

Marx contends that the secret to understanding ancient European society is to acknowledge that conflict between freemen and slaves on the one hand, and commoners (plebeians) and nobles (patricians) on the other. Most everywhere there existed, in Marx's words, "a complicated arrangement of society into

|various orders." During European feudalism, Marx points to the existence of "feudal lords, vassals, guild-masters, journeymen, apprentices, serfs" to illustrate the diversity of rungs on the social ladder. What makes each of these classes different is not personal traits, but instead a specific group's relation to the means of production. In the Middle Ages, Who controlled the land? (nobles) Who grew comfortable off the work of their serfs? (nobles) Who was forced to work, whether by law (serfs) or by necessity (freemen)?

What all these previous societies had in common was that "oppressor and oppressed, stood in constant opposition to one another." This conflict was often hidden behind a curtain of pretended deference, yet sometimes the fight would break out into the open. This battle between different segments of society "each time ended in a revolutionary reconstitution of society at large, or in the common ruin of the contending classes." Marx rejects the commonly held myth praising the harmony among classes, from the "good king" all the way down to the "faithful serf." Marx urges the reader to rediscover past class struggles, whether they take the form of open rebellion or more covert subversion of the established social order.

The class struggle did not disappear with the establishment of capitalism and bourgeois society. On the contrary, Marx saw a new set of classes fighting for control of society. The varied, complex, and confusing array of ancient and feudal orders was replaced by a much more simplified class system. He believed society was "more and more splitting up into two great hostile camps, into two great classes directly facing each other: bourgeoisie and proletariat." Those who own property, the capitalists, command those who do not, the workers.

This is not to say that Marx saw these two as the only important social classes in modern society. Rather obviously there were others, most notably the peasantry, which at the time of the *Manifesto* represented the vast majority of humanity, even in industrializing European societies. There also existed a vast army of servants such as cooks, house cleaners, coachmen, and butlers who worked for the rich but not as part of the industrial working class. At first glance, these facts would seem to render Marx's contention about "two great camps" erroneous but that would miss the crux of the Marxian argument.

Marx contended that classes other than the bourgeoisie and the proletariat were in a long period of historical decline. As industrialization continued, more and more members of the rural population would be pushed off the land and into factories, while technology would reduce the need for servants, who also would find themselves at factory gates seeking employment. Steadily improving technology would produce more and more food, and the traditional social importance of the countryside would go into a terminal decline and become little more than a distant memory. Of more importance to Marx was that, as formerly independent craftsmen and farmers were deprived of their livelihoods, they would be forced by and large to become wage workers within the industrial system. The once proud shoemaker, tailor, and blacksmith would ultimately find their crafts mechanized, as the weavers had experienced in the 1840s.

Dialectical Method

As is often noted, Marx took from Hegel the concept of dialectics. This concept has been much misunderstood, and at times even deliberately distorted. Hegel had argued that the world changes through conflict of ideas that are constantly in motion. Marx took this idea and, as it is often put, stood Hegel on his head to create a dialectics based not on ideas but material forces. Since the only constant is change, the world is always in the process of both dying and being reborn at the same time. On a map, there may be a river pictured as if it were a unchanging physical feature, but we know that rivers are constantly changing in their courses and in their ecology. It has been said you can't step into the same river twice since it is always in the process of change. Everything changes through the dynamic interaction of forces.

The most important aspect of dialectics, for Marx, was the application of this theoretical tool toward the study of human society. In doing so, he argued that all history is the history of classes in opposition to each other, and the resolution of these conflicts results in qualitative new types of civilizations. This change is not merely a matter of slow changes, since at a certain point a degree of change turns into a complete break from the past. In other words, social struggles are resolved by a new set of human relations.

An analogy from the physical world is how water may be raised or lowered in temperature within a certain range without changing its nature, but when water rises to a certain temperature it boils, and when it falls below another temperature it freezes. To use another example from the physical world, if one views animals non-dialectically it means seeing each species as unique and immutable, in perfect harmony with its environment. If Darwin's theory of evolution has any validity, it is clear that species are constantly changing or evolving through conflict with other forces in nature. Marx contended that these insights were all the more true of humans because all people are themselves full of contradictions. The radical conclusion he drew from this is that a dialectical approach sees history as change not stability. This means, of course, that capitalism is not the end of history, but rather just one moment on the road of human development. Such insights are why Marx's use of dialectics is so revolutionary.

Theory of Labor Exploitation

It is useful to explore exactly what Marx meant by "bourgeoisie" and "proletariat," since he saw them as the only two essential classes of the future. By bourgeois, Marx meant the class that owned the means of production and transportation. Their wealth ultimately came less from clever business deals and more from paying workers less than the value of what those workers produced. In a working day, the production costs of one worker might be five dollars of raw material and another five dollars in energy, fixed costs of production, and so on. That worker might be paid five dollars for the day's labor. Yet, the product altogether might fetch thirty dollars on the wholesale market. The difference between the cost of production (fifteen dollars) and the market value (thirty dollars) is what Marx called surplus value. Modern economists have a concept somewhat similar called "value added." This would not necessarily be profit. Some money might be spent to pay for advertising, or the products might pile up in a warehouse in the event of a depression. Still, Marx charged that the owners were exploiting the workers by taking much of the value of the workers' labor for themselves.

The proletariat, in contrast, is the group that must sell their labor-power in return for wages. They were compelled to do this because without those wages they could not eat, find shelter, or otherwise support themselves. They might prosper to a limited extent when business was good and work abundant, but be out on the street when the boon turned to bust.

When speaking of "private property," Marx did not have in mind personal possessions. Karl Marx, a hopeless cigar addict, joked that the tobacco factory might belong to the bourgeoisie, but once he bought his cigars to smoke they were his. Put differently, property that exploited labor in hope of a profit was completely different than the cloth cap a common worker might own. The first was private property in the sense Marx used the phrase, and the latter was personal property.

It has been argued by liberals and social reformers that the cooperation of labor and capital has been what moved societies forward. Marx's response was that a factory owner, no matter how nice personally, is forced to keep production costs (and thus wages) as low as possible. Many production costs such as energy, raw materials, or transportation were beyond the control of an individual capitalist. The one and most important cost that the bourgeois might hope to control was labor. Therefore, the capitalist seeks the lowest wages possible. Workers for their part would naturally seek to receive more instead of less money for their labor. This sets the bottom line of the class struggle: The boss wishes to pay less, while the employee wants more.

As in any struggle, this class war has its ups and downs, advances and retreats; even temporary truces. Despite all of this, for Marx the struggle is always there, even if hidden beneath the surface of a seemingly satisfied society. Few would seriously argue that classes have disappeared in the twenty-first century. If anything, the world has returned to the point where the jest of a French social critic that it is the majesty of the law that "prohibits rich and poor alike from begging in the public streets and sleeping under bridges" is as apt as when first penned in the nineteenth century. But wasn't the spread of liberal democracy going to eliminate such vast inequalities?

Role of the State

Karl Marx developed a theory to help explain why the spread of liberalism and democracy has had so little impact on social stratification. Many theorists have argued that government (the state) is a neutral vessel filled with the political content of the elected officials and through them presumably the people. Thus, once formal political democracy was achieved, the state would change automatically in response to the needs of the populace. Marx maintained, however, that even the most liberal state under capitalism remains little more than the executive committee of big business. Free elections under capitalism, which so many in the nineteenth century saw as the transformative development, proved to be perfectly compatible with extreme class inequality.

The "Dictatorship of the Proletariat" was a concept that Marx and Engels promoted to explain how a transition from capitalism to socialism might occur. This accepts the limitations of civil liberties among those opposed to the revolution during a transition period. The problem has always been raised that there would be a tendency to keep any system of power established during this period. Thus, there is a tension between Marx's commitment to popular democracy and his belief in the need for a firm hand during a revolutionary crisis. For him, if not his critics, this problem is solved by the experience of the Commune that both expanded democracy for the masses while restricting the rights of the counter-revolutionaries.

As Marx commented in *The Civil War in France*, every governmental apparatus is designed to serve a certain dominant class. In the Middle Ages, kingdoms were organized around principles that would support feudalism. In the contemporary era, the governmental structure is organized to serve the capitalists. Many modern constitutions codify property rights, even at the cost of human rights. By the twenty-first century, even the most democratic of nations have seen the increased power of money to "buy" elections. Marx commented on how governments find themselves with only limited power as long as capitalists control the economy. Although he considered it to be the first workers' government, in his critique of the Paris Commune, Marx lamented the Communards' failure to seize the Bank of France, which might have won them a stronger bargaining position. By ignoring the financial basis of its opponents' power, the Commune condemned itself to an early death.

At the same time, Marx viewed the Paris Commune as a great achievement, as it demonstrated that the old state machinery could not merely be seized and utilized. To establish a true people's government, an entirely new and more democratic structure was introduced in Paris. The Commune introduced such drastic changes as immediate recall of elected officials, rotation of officials, limitation of politicians' pay to that of average people, and a host of other innovations. Although short-lived, the Paris Commune gave Marx and Engels an example of what real democracy might look like.

In his support for Abraham Lincoln and the Union during the American Civil War, Marx stressed that slavery could only be abolished by going beyond the limits of a constitution that gave human bondage a protected position. As Marx hoped, Lincoln began the process of freeing the slaves in opposition to a state structure and a constitution that privileged slavery. That is, Lincoln really had no constitutional right to abolish slavery, particularly not by executive decree. Since Marx's time numerous so-called socialist or left governments have held office only to renounce their platforms because of constitutional constraints, fear of capital flight, or worries about military action. Marx understood that there was a huge difference between being in office and being in power. He argued that most of those "in power" were not technically "in office," and vice versa. Returning to the twenty-first century, Marx would not consider most governments—be it China or the United States—democratic. For Marx, democracy was more than constitutions, elections, and a formal apparatus of government. Democracy would have to serve the mass of the population in practice not just in theory.

Before Marx, many utopian thinkers had regarded the state as, at best, a secondary concern. Understanding that the state had to be addressed was a key insight for Marx. Even reformers who do not strive to replace the existing apparatus acknowledge the centrality of the state in political life. Moreover, unlike his anarchist critics, Marx argued that a state apparatus would be needed for the foreseeable future. The question was what kind of state? In the brief experience of the Paris Commune, he caught a glimpse of how a state could be established that was democratic and genuinely inclusive toward the mass of the population. Marx hoped that over time government would become less and less a repressive force and more and more an agency helping society. In his words, the state would ultimately "wither away." This would not happen overnight and would be a long and difficult process; the time it would take was impossible to predict ahead of time. In this, Marx was on solid historical footing, in that he realized that it had taken centuries for feudalism to evolve out of ancient slave societies and then for capitalism to emerge from medieval society.

Acceptance of the Industrial Revolution

A common misconception that arises from time to time, and may even become accepted wisdom for some, is that Karl Marx was opposed to industrialism and the new technology it produced. Such a one-sided and partial view looks only at Marx protesting certain aspects of the Industrial Revolution and from there leaps to the conclusion that he was opposed to technological progress as a whole. Nothing could miss the mark more widely than casting Marx as a backward looking or utopian thinker. Although these opinions did exist in certain parts of the workers' movement, Marx and Engels had nothing but contempt for them.

The *Communist Manifesto*, to cite their most famous example, is often called a love poem to the industrial bourgeoisie. The latter are credited with positively changing the world more in a generation than other classes did over long centuries. What Marx criticized was not the industrial system itself, but rather the manner it was being used. As early as 1845, Marx cites with obvious approval the views of the economist Sismondi strongly indicating that his views were identical:

> My objections are not to machines, not to inventions, not to civilization,
> but only to the modern organization of society, which deprives the working

man of any property other than his hands and gives him no guarantee against competition, of which he will inevitably become a victim. Suppose that all people share equally in the product of the labor in which they have participated, and then every technical invention will in all possible cases be a blessing for all of them.

It was never technological advance or machines that Marx opposed. It was how new methods of production were being used to exploit the common people, whose toil and labor always far outpaced their meager rewards. When Marx spoke of exploitation, he simply meant that workers did not receive or control the value of the production their labor-power created. Most fundamentally, Marx supported the Industrial Revolution because he believed it set the stage for a better, kinder, more truly human society. By advancing technological change, the bourgeoisie was creating the material possibility for a more equal society. Marx reasoned that class stratification, oppression, ignorance, and poverty had all developed because all previous societies had a relative shortage of goods and services. Thus, those with power endeavored to make sure that their families got the lion's share of any surplus, even if it meant hardship for the common people. As industrialism unfolded, it became clear that ever more productive technologies would radically increase the amount of goods and services potentially available. For Marx, this meant that the problem was no longer an absolute shortage where someone would have to suffer. Instead, the bourgeoisie held back production and even technology to maximize profits.

If the technology of the Industrial Revolution could be unleashed for the benefit of the entire planet, Marx thought it would solve many of the problems that had plagued humanity, such as hunger, poverty, illiteracy, and disease. This would not come about because of the charity of the rich, but rather as an outgrowth of the industrial capitalist society. In Notebook VI of *The Grundrisse*, Marx comments on how the drive of the industrialist for profit will ultimately reduce the amount of labor needed and reduce his wage bill. The unexpected result will be that capital "quite unintentionally reduces human labor, expenditure of energy, to a minimum. This will rebound to the benefit of emancipated labor, and is the condition of its emancipation."

It is a tribute to Marx that, when there was so much knee-jerk opposition to industrialization on the one hand, and blind acceptance no matter the human cost on the other, he was able to develop a nuanced interpretation. In his thinking and actions, he refused to reject the Industrial Revolution as many reactionaries, religious fanatics, and rural anarchists did. Instead, he pointed to the wonderful advances of industrialism, yet, Marx never let his enthusiasm for change blind him to the oppressive and exploitative nature of capitalism.

* * * *

Marx was, as are all people, deeply flawed and doubtlessly wrong about many things. Still, he made a major contribution to world history by supporting a more just version of modern industrial society. Marx never lived to use e-mail, notebook computers, cell phones, or visit Facebook. Not withstanding his critique of bourgeois exploitation, he almost certainly would have approved of many of these new tools but then demanded a radical transformation of that very same technology so it would better serve the average person and the common good. Agree or disagree with Karl Marx, and a strong case can be made for either viewpoint, it is hard to ignore his critique of industrial capitalism, or forget his dream of a more cooperative, just, and peaceful world.

Nor can we forget that the vision of revolution articulated by Marx helped rally common people to win concessions and social reforms. Likewise, his predictions of continued economic turmoil and the dangers of unchecked rule by the corporate elite would appear to have turned out to be prophetic. As the world has become a smaller place through the process of globalization, his fear of misled industrialization and warnings about exploitation seem, to many, as timely as they were in nineteenth-century Europe.

Afterword: Marx's Doubtful Heirs

Karl Marx has left his mark on the world, directly or indirectly, in innumerable ways. Within the social sciences, many of his ideas have led to changes in the way some intellectuals look at their field of study. One needs only to cite a few examples to illustrate this point. Many sub-fields of sociology, such as alienation theory and social stratification studies, have been influenced by Marx's concepts. Among historians, the influence of Karl Marx is such that entire new fields have arisen that reject the prior emphasis on the actions of "great men." Economics continues to have an embattled but fierce group of partisans who accept at least some of Marx's basic assumptions. Fields as diverse as philosophy, anthropology, and even art have individuals who claim inspiration from Marx's writings.

Nor are Marx's views so out of touch with at least the rhetoric of some mainstream leaders. In the summer of 2009, one such leader issued a long statement attacking social injustice. Attacking problems that Marx repeatedly commented on, we hear a plea that we prevent "economic choices [from causing] disparities in wealth to increase." The same statement argued that food and water are a universal human right while bemoaning the weakness of trade unions. These unions "experience greater difficulty in carrying out the task of representing the interests of workers . . . [because governments yield to economic pressure to] limit the freedom or negotiating capacity of labor." The statement was titled *Caritas in Veritate*. The author was Pope Benedict XVI.

Of great importance are the political parties and movements that have claimed affinity with the German thinker and activist. Critics hostile to Marx and his thought often point selectively to only examples where "Marxism" is used to justify injustice. In contrast, those authors sympathetic to Marx point to his more democratic self-proclaimed followers. The truth is that Karl Marx and his writings have been used in the generations since his death by a bewildering assortment of very different political types. These can range from a cynical mass murderer looking for a fig leaf to cover his brutality to devout Christian recruiting volunteers to feed the homeless. Marx was frustrated that he could not control the use of his name while he was alive, how much worse it is for him in death. He and Engels can no more fairly be charged with Stalin's gulag than Martin Luther can be indicted as the architect of the Holocaust or St. Peter blamed for the Spanish Inquisition.

We can trace several significant schools of political practice that *claim* to be inspired by Marx. Every historical context is unique and to generalize is always to risk blunders. Still, some generalizations are useful to reveal the broad outlines of the movements that, to one degree or another, claim descent from Marx. These generalizations could be organized into any number of categories but for the sake of simplicity let us use just three: (1) social democracy, (2) Stalinism and third-world variants, (3) revolutionary groupings. What all these people tended to get from Marx was the notion of inevitability. That is, Marx's writings can easily be interpreted as saying that capitalism is doomed and socialism is inevitable. Scholars still debate whether this is what he actually thought but no matter it is a problem that has continued to influence those who study his work.

The first group is the social democrats and their affiliated labor organizations. The most important of these organizations are the direct political descendants of socialists claiming, to one degree or another, to follow Marx during his lifetime. These parties organized themselves into the Socialist International in 1889 with the participation of Engels and Eleanor Marx. Among descendants are the Social Democratic Party of Germany (SPD), the French Socialist Party, the Spanish Socialist Workers Party, and various social democratic parties throughout Scandinavia. Moreover, there exist social democratic parties in this tradition in most nations of the world.

Most of these parties supported World War I and caused their radical members to split off and form more left-wing groups. Over time, these parties became more white collar and less blue collar in their electoral support. They gradually abandoned the goal of abolishing or even drastically changing capitalism. Instead, they became more and more parties of popular reform. Even as they drifted further and further from their Marxist origins, these parties often continued to pay lip service to Marx for decades. For instance, the SPD in Germany did not officially remove the Marxist parts of their program until 1959. In France, a socialist prime minister of the late twentieth century quoted Marx and his son-in-law Paul Lafargue's *Right to be Lazy* in his arguments for a shorter workweek.

The European, particularly Scandinavian, social democratic parties point to universal health care, free education, a shorter workweek, higher life expectancy, more gender equality, and far less social inequality than countries like Japan or the United States as evidence of socialist roots. Critics jeer that the social democrats have only managed capitalism for the bourgeoisie. They respond that they have improved the life of the people. For all their moderation, the social democrats still honor Marx. In Trier, Germany, they have turned his childhood home into a museum. One suspects that the honors shown Marx would most likely have annoyed him. But, who knows? Maybe Marx would have like to find streets bearing his name along with the occasional postage stamp or coin.

The social democratic descendants of Marx have mainly been successful in industrialized societies. In underdeveloped nations, the results have been different where many dictatorships have come into being. The most important of these was Josef Stalin, whose forcible industrialization of Russia was achieved at a staggering human cost. Stalin took from Marx his hatred of the bourgeoisie and the need to industrialize, but he had only contempt for democracy. It can be argued that Stalin never even understood Marx but used his name as a way of justifying the ruthless measures he took to gain and maintain power. This is a historical experience that has greatly contributed to Marx getting a bad reputation.

After World War II, the Russian army occupied Eastern Europe after throwing back Hitler's Nazi armies. Within a matter of a few years, Stalin had imposed dictators in the occupied countries who were cut from the same cloth as he was. To excuse the expansion of autocratic powers, Stalin dusted off some quotes from Marx and stated that the Russian occupation was carried out to further workers' solidarity. Ironically, Marx had predicted revolution in industrialized nations like Germany, England, or the United States. On the other hand, he had contempt for Russian "backwardness." The Stalin model of development had great appeal for some in underdeveloped nations. The goal of rapid industrialization, with the hope of Soviet aid, led many dictatorships to declare themselves "Marxist." This "Marxism" often occurred after the local autocrat had his aid request turned down by the West and so turned to the Soviet Union for assistance.

An important variation of this Stalinist trend is the Chinese version. Named after the leader of the Chinese Communist Party at the time he seized power, Maoism uses the name of Marx but pays little attention to any of his ideas. For Mao, workers were secondary to the peasantry in underdeveloped nations. Anything Marx and Engels would have recognized as democracy was foreign to Maoist doctrine. With time, Mao made his peace with the United States under President Nixon, and China swiftly moved toward being economically allied to the United States and building low-cost consumer goods for stores like WalMart.

A final tendency is what we might call revolutionary groupings. These individuals and organizations see themselves as continuing Marx's legacy by fighting for the abolition of capitalism by promoting democracy in the working class. Many of these came to Marx through the vision of exiled Russian revolutionary Leon Trotsky, who was murdered on Stalin's orders. These groups tend to attack the social democrats and Stalinists as having "sold out" the workers struggle. These individuals differ greatly. At one extreme, some have an almost religious allegiance to Marx while others use his name as shorthand for their radical viewpoint. Although smaller in number and influence than either the social democrats or the Stalinists, these revolutionaries have strong political influence particularly in times of crisis and especially among intellectuals.

They often help lead protests or social movements far larger than their size would suggest.

Maybe the best way to sum up those who have claimed Marx is to conclude they are all, to one degree or another, selective. Many, including Karl Kautsky, V.I. Lenin, and Fidel Castro, have found things in the writings of Karl Marx that support some position of theirs. When Marx's ideas contradict them, they will ignore them. European former communists, socialists, and social democrats are pretty much all the same in this regard. In short, with most political leaders, pragmatism takes place over purity. The latest election poll takes precedence over anything Marx wrote. Power has logic of its own. So it was in Marx's time as well.

Chronology

1818
May 5 — Karl Marx born to Heinrich and Henriette Marx in Trier, western Germany

1820
November 28 — Frederick Engels born in Barmen

1830
October — Marx enters Friedrich-Wilhelm Gymnasium (high school) in Trier

1835
September 24 — Marx graduates from Friedrich-Wilhelm Gymnasium
October 15 — Karl Marx begins the study of law at Bonn University

1836
Mid-October — Marx moves to Berlin to study law

1838
May 10 — Heinrich Marx dies in Trier

1841
March 30 — Karl Marx ends his studies at Berlin University
April 15 — Marx receives his doctor's degree from the Jena University philosophical faculty

1842
April — Marx begins to work on newspaper, *Rheinische Zeitung*
October — Marx moves to Cologne and becomes editor-in-chief of *Rheinische Zeitung*
November — Engels meets Marx for the first time

1843
March 17 — Marx stops being editor of *Rheinische Zeitung*
June 19 — Jenny von Westphalen marries Karl Marx

1844

February	First *German-French Yearbook* appears in Paris
May 1	The first daughter, Jenny, is born to the Marxes
June 4–6	Revolt of Silesian weavers
August 28	Engels visits Marx in Paris marking the beginning of their friendship and collaboration

1845

February 5	Marx expelled from Paris, moves to Brussels
End February	First joint Marx–Engels work, *The Holy Family* appears in Frankfurt am Main
April	Engels moves to Brussels from Barmen to join Marx
September 26	Marx's daughter Laura is born

1846

March 30	Marx and Engels set up a Communist Correspondence Committee in Brussels
May	*The German Ideology* is finished but publication in Germany is halted by censorship regulations
August 15	At request of Communist Correspondence Committee, Engels moves to Paris

1847

January	Marx and Engels join the League of the Just
June	First Congress of Communist League in London
July	*The Poverty of Philosophy* is written by Marx in response to Proudhon's *The Philosophy of Poverty*
August 5	Communist League is set up in Brussels
November 29	Marx and Engels attend second congress of the Communist League in London and are asked to draft League's program

1848

January 31	Engels expelled from Paris goes to Brussels
February 22	Revolution breaks out in France
February 24	*Communist Manifesto*, program of the Communist League, appears in London
March 4	Marx expelled from Brussels moves with family to Paris
March 13	Outbreak of revolution in Vienna
March 18	Fighting on barricades in Berlin
March 21	Engels arrives in Paris
April	Marx and Engels leave Paris and go to Germany
May 18	German National Assembly meets in Frankfurt am Main
May 22	Prussian Constituent Assembly gathers in Berlin
May 31	First *Neue Rheinische Zeitung* appears with Marx as editor-in-chief

June 23–26	Uprising of workers in Paris
November 8	Start of counterrevolutionary putsch in Prussia

1849

February 7–8	Marx on trial for being editor of *Neue Rheinische Zeitung*
March 28	National Assembly in Frankfurt am Main adopts a German constitution
May	Armed uprising in Dresden, the Palatinate, Baden, and Prussian Rhine to defend constitution against counterrevolution
May 19	Last issue of *Neue Rheinische Zeitung* appears
June 3	Marx goes to Paris for Democratic Central Committee
August 26	Marx expelled from Paris, arrives in London
November 10	Engels arrives in London

1850

May	Wilhelm Liebknecht meets Marx after Liebknecht is expelled from Switzerland
July	Marx begins systematic study of political economy
November	Engels moves to Manchester (England) and works for family firm of Ermen & Engels

1851

Fall	Marx and Engels begin to write for *New York Daily Tribune*

1852

May 19	*The Eighteenth Brumaire of Louis Bonaparte* appears in New York
October 4	Trial of arrested members of the Communist League in Cologne
November 17	London Communist League dissolves itself at Marx's suggestion

1853

January	*Disclosures About the Communist Trial in Cologne* appears in Basle
October 4	Crimean war begins

1854

December	Marx writes for *Neue Oder Zeitung*

1855

January 16	Marx's daughter Eleanor is born

1859

May	Marx and Engels write for *Das Volk* which appears in London
June 11	*Critique of Political Economy* appears in Berlin

1860

December 1   *Herr Vogt* is printed in London

1861   Civil War begins in the United States

1862

July   Wilhelm Liebknecht moves to London

September 24   Bismarck becomes Prussian prime minister

1863

January 22   Start of revolt in Poland against Russian Tsar

May 23   General German Workers' Association founded in Leip-
                    zig with Ferdinand Lassalle as president

November 30   Marx's mother dies in Trier

1864

February 1   Prussia and Austria declare war on Denmark

August 31   Death of Ferdinand Lassalle

September 28   Founding of International Working Men's Association in
                    London

November 24   *Inaugural Address* and *Provisional Rules* of International
                    Working Men's Association, drafted by Marx, pub-
                    lished in London

1865   Marx's *Value, Price and Profit* appears

1866

June 16   War between Prussia and Austria

September 3–8   Congress of International Working Men's Association in
                    Geneva

1867

September 2–8   Congress of International Working Men's Association in
                    Lausanne

September 14   First volume of *Capital* is published

1868

April 2   Laura Marx marries Paul Lafargue

September 5–7   Conference of German Workers' Association decides to
                    join International Working Men's Association

1869

August 7–9   Founding congress of the Social Democratic Workers'
                    Party in Eisenach

September 6–11   Congress of International Working Men's Association in
                    Basle

1870

July 19	France declares war on the North German States
July 19–23	Marx writes *First Address of the General Council on the German-French War*
September 1–2	Battle of Sedan. Defeat of French army
September 9	General Council of the International approves *Second Address on the German-French War* drafted by Marx
September 20	Engels moves to London

1871

January 18	Proclamation of the German Kaiser Reich in Versailles
March 18–May 28	Paris Commune
May 30	Marx's *The Civil War in France*, endorsed by General Council of the International
September 17–23	Conference of the International in London under leadership of Marx and Engels

1872

September	Marx and Engels at the Hague Congress as delegates to the International
September 6	The Hague Congress decides to transfer the seat of the General Council to New York
October 10	Marx's daughter Jenny marries French socialist Charles Longuet

1875

May 5	Marx sends his *Marginal Notes on the Program of the German Workers' Party* to German socialist leaders
May 22–27	Unity congress in Gotha results in the founding of the Socialist Workers' Party of Germany

1876 Death of Mikhail Bakunin

1877

Until August	Marx works on the tenth chapter of the second section of Engels' book, *Herr Eugen Duhring's Revolution in Science*
April 24	Russian-Turkish war

1878

October 19	German Reichstag (Congress) passes the antisocialist law.

1879

September 17–18	Engels sends a circular letter drafted by him and Marx to August Bebel, Wilhelm Liebknecht, and other German socialist leaders

1880

Early May	Marx helps Engels, Jules Guesde, and Paul Lafargue with the program of the French Workers' Party
August 20–23	Underground congress of the Socialist Workers' Party of Germany in Wyden, Switzerland
December 9–16	August Bebel visits Marx and Engels for the first time in London

1881

July 26–August 16	Marx and Jenny Marx visited their daughter Jenny in vicinity of Paris
December 2	Marx's wife, Jenny, dies in London

1882

February 9–early October	Marx takes a journey that includes Algiers, France, and Switzerland, and he visits his daughters Jenny and Laura

1883

January 11	Marx's daughter Jenny dies in Paris
March 14	Marx dies in London
March 17	Karl Marx is buried at Highgate Cemetery in London

1895

August 5	Death of Engels

Significant Works

Critique of Hegel's Philosophy of Right [1843]
On the Jewish Question [1843]
Contribution to a Critique of Hegel's Philosophy of Right: Introduction [1843]
Notes on James Mill [1844]
Economic and Philosophical Manuscripts [1844]
Theses on Feuerbach [1845]
The German Ideology (with Engels) [1845–1846]
The Poverty of Philosophy [1846–1847]
Wage-Labour and Capital [1847]
The Communist Manifesto (with Engels) [1847–1848]
The Eighteenth Brumaire of Louis Bonaparte [1852]
Grundrisse [1857–1858]
A Contribution to the Critique of Political Economy [1859]
Wages, Price and Profit [1865]
Capital, vol. 1 [1867]
The Civil War in France [1871]
Critique of the Gotha Programme [1875]
Ethnological Notebooks [1879–1880]

Glossary of Some Important People in Marx's Life

What follows is by necessity brief and incomplete. Many important but well-known people, such as Adam Smith, have consciously been excluded. There are many more complete and encompassing biographical works on this topic. See, for example, the resources of the Marxist Internet Archive, cited in "A Note on the Sources" section.

Aveling, Edward (1849–1898)

A native of London, Aveling trained as a medical doctor and taught science with particular interest in Darwin's theories. He was still legally married when he met Eleanor Marx, the youngest daughter of Karl Marx. Although Aveling could not legally marry, he lived with Eleanor until her suicide in 1898. Aveling and Eleanor worked together on interests from theatre to politics. Though respected for his intellect, a cloud hung over his reputation after his involvement in a series of financial scandals in various organizations. Edward Aveling is credited with the translating the first English edition of *Capital*, vol. 1. He died a few months after Eleanor's suicide, for which he was widely blamed.

Bakunin, Mikhail (1814–1876)

In his youth Bakunin was a Hegelian, but he is best known as one of the fathers of anarchism. In 1848, he took part in the uprising in Dresden and was arrested the following year and sent back to Russia. Following the death of the Tsar Nicholas I, Bakunin was exiled to Siberia in 1857. Four years later, he escaped from Siberia and made his way to London. Bakunin became a member of the League of Peace and Freedom. At the Berne Congress of the League (1868), he and his supporters were in a minority and seceded from the League, establishing their own International Alliance of Socialist Democracy. In 1869, this Alliance became affiliated with the International Working Men's Association (IWMA), also known as the First International. Bakunin and his supporters fought with Marx within the International. The impossibility of resolving this conflict was one of the reasons Marx and Engels moved the IWMA to the United States.

Bebel, August (1840–1913)

Trained as a cabinet maker, Bebel became a radical and helped found the German Social Democratic Party with Wilhelm Liebknecht in 1869. Bebel was elected to the North German Reichstag in 1867 and in 1872 sentenced with Liebknecht to two years imprisonment for opposing the Franco-German War. At a unity congress in Gotha in 1875, his party merged with those who had followed Lassalle. Until his death the year before World War I, Bebel remained the unquestioned leader of this united party. While his fiery parliamentary speeches were part of the legend of German social democracy, he also wrote a number of influential works including his *From My Life* and *Woman under Socialism*.

Bismarck, Otto von (1815–1898)

As the chief architect of the unification of Germany in 1871, Bismarck dominated the German and European political scene from 1862 to 1890 as chancellor, first of Prussia and then of a united Germany. The new German Reich was dominated by Prussia and its royal family, the Hohenzollerns. In a futile hope of crushing the left, Bismarck supported antisocialist laws that banned the Social Democratic Party, mass workers' organizations, and the workers' press. He was also unsuccessful in his attack on political Catholicism. Bismarck was finally forced from office by Kaiser (Emperor) Wilhelm II in March 1890.

Blanc, Louis (1811–1882)

A French reformist, socialist, and historian, Blanc denied that class contradictions under capitalism were antagonistic, opposed violent revolution, and wanted to win a compromise with the bourgeoisie. He is best known for attempting to set up national workshops to establish full employment during the 1848 revolution. Later, he was mocked by revolutionaries who considered his politics to be opportunist and conciliatory.

Blanqui, Louis-Auguste (1805–1881)

Blanqui was uninterested in economic, social, or historical theory. A dedicated revolutionary socialist he spent almost a third of a century in prison. Blanqui believed a successful worker's revolution could only be led by a small group of disciplined revolutionary workers.

Beginning in 1827, he took an active part in student demonstrations against the restored Bourbon monarchy. As a member of the Société des Amis du Peuple, Blanqui was first imprisoned in 1831 and again in 1836. As a reaction to this police persecution, Blanqui concluded that only extremely disciplined workers could achieve revolution. Blanqui organized the Society of the Seasons (Société des Saisons) and attempted an armed insurrection on May 12, 1839, in Paris. Isolated from the Parisian workers, five hundred revolutionaries were slaughtered in less than two days of fighting, and Blanqui was caught and sentenced to life imprisonment on the island of Mont-Saint-Michel.

Released shortly before the Revolution of 1848, he returned to Paris, and created a new reformist society. The conservative government that was elected to the Constituent Assembly used Blanqui as a political scapegoat. He was sentenced to ten years imprisonment on the false charge of having participated in a demonstration. Released from prison in 1859, he returned to organizing, was again arrested in 1861, and held until he escaped to Belgium in 1865. His all-too frequent stays in prison earned him the name *l'enfermé* (the locked-up one).

After the beginning of the French Civil War of 1871, the Paris Commune was elected, with Blanqui as president. The conservative government of Thiers refused to release Blanqui, despite his election. After tens of thousands of workers were massacred in Paris by government troops ordered to suppress the Commune, Blanqui was kept in prison. In April 1879, he was elected deputy for Bordeaux, but the government refused to recognize the election. After public protests, the government concluded that releasing the seventy-four year-old man would be the lesser evil. Blanqui continued to agitate for socialism until he died at seventy-six years.

Dana, Charles Anderson (1819–1897)

Journalist who was the editor of the *New York Daily Tribune* while Marx was contributing articles to that paper.

Danielson, Nicolai Frantzevich (1844–1918)

This Russian author was the translator of *Capital*, vol. 1.

Darwin, Charles (1809–1882)

The scientist credited with the evolutionary theory of the development of the animal world, the struggle for existence, adaptation, and the "survival of the fittest," his work analyses the transformation of organisms. Marx was quite taken with Darwin and attempted to dedicate *Capital* to him. In many ways, Marx and Engels saw Darwin's work as complimentary to their own, although there is no evidence that Darwin agreed with this sentiment. What they did share was a passionate hatred of slavery and all other forms of human bondage. This view shaped Darwin's work as much as Marx.

Lafargue, Paul (1841–1911)

Paul Lafargue was born in 1842 in Santiago, Cuba, of mixed race. As a young boy, he moved to France where he studied medicine and first became involved in politics. As a French delegate to the IWMA, he became friendly with Marx and Engels and his views approached those of Marx. Married in 1868 to Laura Marx, Marx's second daughter, the Lafargues began several decades of political work together, financially supported by Engels.

Lafargue was one of the Marxist leaders of the French Workers' Party. During the Franco-Prussian War of 1870–1871, he carried on political work in Paris and Bordeaux. After the fall of the Commune, Lafargue fled first to Spain and then to London before returning to France. He was an influential speaker and the author of numerous works including the humorous, *"The Right to Be Lazy."* Upon reaching seventy, in 1911, Paul and Laura Lafargue committed suicide together, having decided they had nothing left to give to the movement that had given their lives meaning.

Lassalle, Ferdinand (1825–1864)

He took part in the French Revolution of 1848 and established the Democratic Socialist Party in Germany. By 1862, Lassalle had proposed a theory (commonly called *Lassalleanism*) espousing the idea that while bourgeois society "guaranteed" all individuals unlimited development of their individual productive forces, the *moral* idea of the proletariat is to render useful service to the community. Lassalle believed that the proletariat represented community, solidarity of interest, and reciprocity of interest. He believed therefore that the cause of the workers is the cause of humanity. When the proletariat gains political supremacy, a higher degree of morality, culture, and science would occur, furthering civilization.

Lassalle believed in the state as Hegel did, as the organ of right and justice. He believed that only through the state could victory be gained and on this basis justified his dealings with the conservative Otto von Bismarck. Marx and Engels referred to him as "an uncertain friend." His vanity may have caused his demise, as he engaged in a duel and was killed by Count von Racowitza on August 31, 1864.

Liebknecht, Wilhelm (1826–1900)

Along with August Bebel, Liebknecht was one of the most important leaders of the German working-class movement. In his youth, he took part in the 1848–1849 revolution and then fled to Switzerland, and later to England. While in England, he became a friend of the Marx family. In 1862, Wilhelm returned to Germany and by 1866, had become founder and leader of the Saxon People's Party, which he, along with Bebel, represented in the North German Reichstag. In 1869, he co-founded the Social-Democratic Workers' Party. A leading orator and popular writer, Liebknecht was consistently re-elected to the German Reichstag (1874–1900). In addition, he was editor of such Social Democratic papers as *Demokratisches Wochenblatt, Volksstaat,* and *Vorwarts.* His son, Karl Liebknecht, played a prominent role in the German Revolution of 1918–1919. Along with Rosa Luxemburg, he founded the German Communist Party and was murdered by rightists in 1919.

Longuet, Charles (1833–1901)

This French radical was a journalist and one-time supporter of Proudhon who married Marx's eldest daughter, *Jenny.* Longuet was a delegate to the Lausanne Congress of the IWMA (1867) and was later a leading member of the Paris

Commune and editor of its official organ. With the defeat of the Commune, he fled to London where he stayed until 1880. Returning to France, Longuet was elected a member of the Paris City Council and worked on the editorial staff of the radical paper *La Justice.*

Marx, Eleanor (Tussy) (1855–1898)

Eleanor, Marx's youngest daughter, was precocious and showed an early interest in politics. She and her two sisters grew up with Marx's storytelling and became drawn to literature. She would later translate several works of literature, as well as become a stage actress. Once engaged to Prosper Lissagary, an exile from the Paris Commune, she later met Edward Aveling in 1883. The couple lived together for the rest of her life. They became members of the Democratic Federation led by Henry Hyndman in the early 1880s. Eleanor wrote in the draft of the program that a revolution was needed to change society.

The Democratic Federation, later renamed the Social Democratic Federation, broke up in 1884 over personalities and fights over internationalism. The Avelings and William Morris then formed the Socialist League, which published a monthly paper called *Commonweal.* Eleanor wrote articles and reviews on women's and other issues as well as a booklet entitled "The Woman Question." In 1886, Eleanor toured in the United States along with Wilhelm Liebknecht fundraising for the German Social Democratic Party and in support of the Haymarket affair victims. While continuing to translate literature and to act, she threw herself into organizing, writing, record-keeping, and speaking for militant trade unions such as the Gas workers' and the Dockers' Union. In 1889, she was a delegate in Paris for the founding of the Second International. Later, she became very involved in organizing her father's papers left to her after the death of Engels. During a period of depression over Aveling's infidelity, in 1889, she committed suicide at the age of forty-three.

Marx, Henriette (1787–1863)

As the mother of Karl Marx, Henriette is best known for having lamented, "If only my son Marx had made capital instead of written about it."

Marx, Jenny von Westphalen (1814–1881)

Karl Marx's wife who was long suffering and devoted to Marx, she made it possible for him to throw himself into study and activism. It was said that when she died, Marx was as good as dead himself.

Marx, Jenny (Jennychen) (1844–1883)

Marx and Jenny Marx's eldest daughter, married to Charles Longuet. In 1870, writing under the name "J. Williams" she drew attention to the Irish struggle by publishing in a French paper revelation of the treatment of the Irish political prisoners by the English. These revelations caused the Gladstone government to conduct an investigation into the situation.

Proudhon, Pierre-Joseph (1809–1865)

This French political economist was acknowledged by Bakunin as the founder of anarchism. Proudhon envisioned a society of independent, self-employed artisans. Coming from humble origins and a printer by trade, Proudhon became well-known throughout Europe by the 1840s. He was the first person to call himself an "anarchist," the word previously having been used as a term of abuse during the French Revolution. He called anarchism "mutualist socialism."

His most famous book was *What Is Property?* (1840) in which he gives the answer, "It is theft." A persistent critic of the status quo, he was nonetheless surprised by the outbreak of street fighting in Paris in February 1848. Determined to set the new republic on the correct course, Proudhon articulated a program of mutual financial cooperation among workers that he believed would transfer control of economic relations from capitalists and financiers to workers. Proudhon opposed insurrection and preached peaceful change, a stance that was in accord with his lifelong stance against violence. He never fully approved of the revolts and demonstrations of 1848. Proudhon faced criticism by conservatives within the National Assembly, especially for the economic reforms that he advanced. Proudhon's proposals were condemned on the floor of the assembly by republican leader Adophpe Thiers.

Proudhon also had a conflict with the new president of the Republic, Louis-Napoleon Bonaparte, which led to his prosecution and imprisonment. Proudhon's attacks became more aggressive in January 1849, and the government responded by having Proudhon sentenced to three years in prison and fined 3000F. Though clearly on the political left, his public quarrels with prominent socialists like Louis Blanc made him unpopular with many radicals.

His stance concerning politics, opposition to universal suffrage followed by his election to the constituent assembly, and insistence that Bonaparte institute reforms "from above" has made it easy to dismiss Proudhon as hopelessly inconsistent. Thrust into politics by the tumultuous events of 1848, Proudhon proved ineffective as a leader. As he himself perceptively noted in 1850, he was basically a "man of polemics, not of the barricades." Still, Proudhon's ideas have continued to have influence up to the present day, especially in France, and the widespread movement for setting up intentional communities have its ideological roots in Proudhon's ideas.

Saint-Simon, Comte (1760–1825)

Comte Claude Henri de Ronvroy Saint-Simon, a French utopian socialist during the French Revolution, was close to the Jacobins. He also participated in the American War of Independence. He subscribed to the materialist current in the Enlightenment and opposed deism, advocated the study of nature, and was one of the first to see that politics was ultimately determined by economics. He advocated the development of the study of the laws governing history as an extension of the natural sciences.

Saint-Simon saw the basic social conflict between "workers" and "idlers." For him workers included manufacturers, merchants, and bankers since they contributed to the economy. He recognized the French Revolution as a class war and in 1816 declared that politics is the science of production. The ideas of Saint-Simon anticipate Marx's of the abolition of the state.

Sismondi, Jean Charles Léonard de (1773–1842)

Jean Charles Léonard de Sismondi was born to an upper-class family in Geneva. In his economic views, Sismondi represented humanitarian protest against the dominant economic thought of his era. Although at first he followed Adam Smith, by 1819, he argued that economics emphasized the means of increasing wealth too much, and using wealth for happiness, too little. Although no socialist, he attacked wealth accumulation both as an end in itself, and because of its adverse effect on the poor. Although Marx thought Sismondi understood the contradictions of capitalism, Marx disagreed with his solutions to the problem which he believed were backward-looking and reactionary.

Weerth, Georg (1822–1856)

Weerth, a poet greatly influenced by Heinrich Heine, was called by Engels "the first and most important poet of the German proletariat." This German revolutionary writer was a member of the "League of Communists," he developed a friendship with Marx and became a contributor to *Deutsche Brusseler Zeitung*. In 1848–1849, Weerth was an editor of the *Neue Rheinische Zeitung*. Weerth took business trips (which were partly political courier journeys) through Holland, Spain, southern, and Central America before dying of tropical fever in Cuba.

Weitling, Wilhelm (1808–1871)

A collaborator of Blanqui, Weiting was one of Germany's first proletarian writers. He may be essentially categorized as a utopian egalitarian socialist. By trade he was a tailor and by choice he became a traveling activist in proletarian movements. Marx criticized the utopian nature of his thought.

Westphalen, Edgar von (1819–1890)

Edgar was the brother of Jenny Marx and became influenced by radical ideas. He tried unsuccessfully to start a utopian community with other German free thinkers in Texas before finally returning to Germany.

Weydemeyer, Joseph (1818–1866)

A Prussian artillery officer and writer, Weydemeyer became, in 1845–1846, a follower of Marx and Engels. As a leading member of the League of Communists in 1849–1851, he became head of its Frankfurt chapter. He visited Marx in Brussels and stayed there for a time while attending Marx's lectures. He was active in the 1848 Revolution, and in 1849–1850 was made one of the "responsible editors" of the *Neue Rheinische Zeitung*. He collaborated in socialist periodicals, such as the *Westphälisches Dampfboot* and the *Neue Rheinische Zei-tung*. In 1851, he emigrated from Germany to America and worked as a journalist while keeping up a frequent correspondence with Marx. During the Civil War, he took part in the struggle against the Southern slave owners as a colonel in the Northern army. His masterful defense of the St. Louis region is often credited with keeping Missouri in the Union.

Glossary of Terms

This is only a brief selection of important terms. There are a number of more complete works such as *A Dictionary of Marxist Thought* and the resources of the Marxist Internet Archive, both cited in "A Note on the Sources" section.

Alienation

This is a situation where people are estranged from the reality around them. Marx saw alienation as particularly strong in modern capitalism because work has become necessary to live. Since wage laborers must sell their ability to work to capitalists for money, the product of labor is alien to the worker. Work becomes a means to an end rather than a human end in and of itself.

Anarchism

Like socialists, anarchists believe in abolishing capitalism. A major difference is that anarchists believe in the immediate destruction of all existing state institutions without any transitional period. While there are many different types of anarchists, all tend to stress the abolition of authority, complete individual liberty, and social equality. Many anarchists believe that to be part of a community is to lose one's freedom.

Capital

Used first in seventeenth-century England in its current meaning, capital is more than just money or wealth. It is money that grows ever larger through a process of circulating through the capitalist economy. Capital is not just money to buy things. It is money that is invested in order to make a profit.

Class

For Marx, class was less determined by annual income and more about a group that shares a common relationship to the means of production. By way of example, a small business owner having a weak year and a worker having a good one might wind up with the same income. Yet, the worker remained subject to the whims of the capitalist while the business owners are their "own bosses."

Commodity

A good or service that is produced for the purpose of exchange is a commodity. What the commodity is does not matter. It could be something basic to life like food or a product designed to satisfy a whim such as designer shoes. Marx saw labor itself as a commodity bought by the capitalist and sold by the worker. This exchange is a fundamental social relation of capitalism.

Dialectics

This is a method of reasoning, promoted by Hegel and adopted by Marx. It is in opposition to formal metaphysical thought that sees all things as having fixed attributes. In dialectics, everything is in constant motion. Everything is moving from something and evolving into something new. It sees everything as having different and contradictory aspects.

Exploitation

In general, exploitation means taking advantage of another's weakness for personal gain. For Marx, however, exploitation is different and is inherent in the capitalist productive process. The capitalist becomes rich by taking the surplus value of the workers' labor-power and combining it with the means of production to create profit. The working class is exploited by the bourgeoisie because laborers are forced to sell their labor at market price (exchange value) while capitalists have access to labors use-value which creates surplus value. Out of this surplus value, not completely dissimilar to the modern concept of "value added," comes profit.

Internationalism

Promoted by Marx, Engels, and the First International, this is the ethical belief that workers of all countries should put the overall interests of the international proletariat above any national or group advantage. First coming into common usage in the 1850s, internationalism meant supporting strikes in foreign countries and refusing to allow national differences to divide workers.

Left-wing / Right-wing

During the French Revolution of 1789, the monarchists and conservatives sat together to the right of the Speaker in the Chamber of Deputies. Seated on the left were the antimonarchical delegates and other radicals. From that time on, left-wing has meant those challenging the status quo and opposing privilege. To be right-wing means support for the existing political system, order, and class structure.

Liberalism

Originally the doctrine of the rising capitalist class against the old feudal lords, this term is now used to mean many different, often contradictory, things. In Marx's day, liberalism stressed individual rights as opposed to social responsibility. Economically, liberalism advocates a "hands off" approach by government. That is to say, liberals believe in the right of property owners to use their economic power without restriction or regulation.

Lumpen proletariat

This term may be translated as "workers in rags." It refers to the sub-class within modern society that is pushed to the margins of society. Among this sector are petty criminals, the perpetually unemployed, beggars, prostitutes, tramps, and all manner of degraded or declassed people. Marx pointed to this group as being manipulated by right-wing demagogues like Louis Bonaparte of France.

Materialism

This is a type of philosophy that uses material reality as its starting point. In contrast to idealism, materialism argues that thoughts are a reflection of reality not vice versa. The real world exists independently of thoughts about it.

Means of Production

The type of technology and raw materials that are used to produce things are the means of production. In different historical periods, there existed various means of production. Hence, the uses by historians of terms like "bronze age," "iron age," or "industrial age." Classes are defined by their relations to the means of production. Some classes own these means (capitalists own factories), while others do not (workers).

Petit or Petty Bourgeoisie

This class is made up of small business owners, well-off farmers, independent crafts people, and certain members of the professional middle class. They have been under pressure since the Industrial Revolution because of their inability to compete against large factories or retail outlets. This class is most common in less industrialized areas of the world. The term is also used to mean a mentality whereby well-off managers or workers identify with the bourgeoisie.

Poverty

This is a situation when basic human needs are not being, or not being fully, met. However, human needs are historically determined. A poor person today might have access to a television, an object beyond the dreams of even the richest noble in the Middle Ages. Yet, that same poor person might be excluded from the advantages others in their society enjoy such as quality health care, education, and opportunities for self-improvement. For Marx, modern poverty amidst plenty was a condition of industrial capitalism, whereas poverty at an earlier time had resulted more from the low level of productivity or bad weather.

Proletariat

Another term for the modern working class, proletariat is the class that lives from the sale of their labor and not from the profits from capital. They sell their time to capitalists but, unlike slaves, they are themselves free. Although often thought to refer only to manual laborers, Marx clearly states that those who work with their brains (white-collar workers) are every bit as much proletarians as those who work with their hands (blue-collar workers).

Social Democracy

A common term since the time of the International Working Men's Association applied to those political parties that were part of the socialist movement. The term was used to distinguish the often pro-Marx groups from anarchists and utopians who often called themselves communist. The idea was also that these parties were fighting to extend democracy from politics to society by the end of capitalism and a workers' democracy. While the term has taken on other meanings since the nineteenth century, it was a label to indicate people supporting democratic socialism.

Surplus Value

That part of the social product over and above what goes to the producers is surplus value. There is a social division of labor in society and those who work receive only a portion of the value they produce. The remaining, or surplus value, is taken by the capitalists who use it to pay rent or buy property, make interest payments on loans, secure raw materials and, of course, profits.

Value

Every commodity has two types of value. In as much as it is a thing that can satisfy a human need or want, a commodity has use-value. Because it is something exchanged in the market, it has exchange value. What is common to all commodities is that their value is the result of human labor.

A Note on the Sources

I. Primary Sources

For those who read English better than German, the best widely available collection of Marx's work is: Karl Marx and Frederick Engels, *Collected Works*, (50 Volumes plus Index Volume), New York: International Publishers, 1975—while a useful collection of the most important works can be found in: Karl Marx and Frederick Engels, *Selected Works* (Three Volumes), Moscow: Progress Publishers, 1975.

For a wonderful collection of work by and about Marx, see also the Marx and Engels Internet Archive at: http://www.marxists.org/archive/marx/index.htm, and for those who read German, http://www.mlwerke.de/me/default.htm has the best collection of Marx's texts in the German language. There are also many other editions, for example those issued by Penguin, McGraw-Hill, or Progress Publishers, that gather together Marx's work available in libraries and book shops. Likewise easy to find are most famous works like *Capital* and the *Communist Manifesto*.

II. Secondary Sources

A. Biographies of Marx

The most readable and enjoyable post–Cold War biography is: Francis Wheen, *Karl Marx: A Life*, New York: W.W. Norton, 2000. This work treats Marx as both a complex thinker and a very humane person. To Wheen, Marx is neither monster nor god but rather a brilliant and contradictory individual who continues to influence society. Another solid work is: David McLellan, *Karl Marx: His Life and Thought*, New York: Harper & Row, 1974. McLellan gives a thoughtful and detailed introduction to Marx's life and thought along with an excellent bibliography. An additional sympathetic yet balanced biography is: Tom Bottomore, *Karl Marx,* London: Blackwell, 1979. A more personal view that still treats Marx's politics in a satisfactory fashion is contained in: Saul K. Padover, *Karl Marx: An Intimate Biography*, New York: McGraw Hill, 1978.

Less satisfactory is Peter Singer, *Marx: A Very Short Introduction*, Oxford: Oxford University Press, 1980. Singer, best known for his book *Animal Liberation*, clearly supports the anti-Marxist anarchists and it shows, particularly in his very weak conclusion which ruins an otherwise useful introduction. An earlier, longer, and even stranger interpretation from a left anti-Marxist perspective is to be had in: Otto Ruhle, *Karl Marx: His Life and Work*, New York: The Viking Press, 1928. This author goes so far as to blame Marx's politics on illness or "organic defect." Heinrich Gemkow et al., *Karl Marx: A Biography*, Dresden (DDR): Verlag Zeit im Bild, 1968 could have been an excellent biography but is marred by the authors need to too closely follow the Soviet Bloc line. Quite different is: Ernesto Che Guevara, *Marx & Engels: A Biographical Introduction*, Melbourne: Ocean Press, 2008. This work is unorthodox but too brief and clearly unfinished to be a major reference.

For a more mainstream treatment of Marx, one can do little better than: Sir Isaiah Berlin, *Karl Marx: His Life and Environment*, New York: Oxford University Press, 1996. First published before World War II, this is the classic non-Marxist treatment of Karl Marx in the English language. A far less satisfactory effort from the right is: Leopold Schwarzchild, *The Red Prussian: The Life and Legend of Karl Marx*, London: H. Hamilton, 1948. More recently, a better argued critical treatment that links Marx's personal problems with his political ideals is: Frank E. Manuel, *A Requiem for Karl Marx*, Cambridge, MA: Harvard University Press, 1995. Manuel sees Marx as a hypocrite who engaged in brutal treatment of his friends and enemies alike.

On the other side of the political universe and first published over a century ago, there is: Franz Mehring, *Karl Marx: The Story of His Life*, New York: Routledge, 2003. Mehring, who was a leader of the left-wing of German socialism and shortly before his death a founder of the German Communist Party, gives a straight forward if clearly partisan account of Marx in great detail. Another work, this time with a Russian slant, that is a classic study is: Boris Nicolaievsky and Otto Maenchen-Helfen, *Karl Marx: Man and Fighter*, London: Methuen Co., Ltd, 1936. The authors claim to "have written the biography of Marx as the strategist of the class struggle."

For a title that focuses more on Marx's personal life, there is: Werner Blumenberg et al., *Karl Marx: An Illustrated Biography*, London: Verso, 1998. The collection of illustrations included is excellent even if Marx's ideas and public life are given short shrift. A short portrait written by one of his son-in-laws has some interesting stories: Paul Lafargue, *Karl Marx-The Man*, New York: New York Labor News, 1972. Another work that stresses the man Marx over Marx the thinker is: Wilhelm Liebknecht, *Karl Marx: Biographical Memoirs*, Chicago: Charles H. Kerr Co., 1908. Although it has little theoretical depth, Liebknecht tells many interesting stories such as his London pub crawl with Marx that almost landed them in jail.

If people would like to see where many of these stories, and others told by different authors, took place, there is: Asa Briggs and John Callow, *Marx in London*, London: Lawrence & Wishart, 2007. Although mainly intended as a guide for walks through London, a great deal can be gotten from the illustrations and descriptions even without visiting the English capital. For those visual learners who prefer graphics to text, there is: RUIS, *Marx for Beginners,* New

York: Pantheon Books, 1976. A good short introduction this work by the famous Mexican cartoonist is mainly, well, cartoons. An additional nontraditional biographical treatment is the play: Howard Zinn, *Marx in Soho*, Cambridge, MA: South End Press, 1999. that has Marx return from the dead to explain his life and ideas to the audience.

B. Interpretations of Marx

There seem to be countless books that aspire to interpret Marx and provide the reader with the "true Marx." Among the better efforts is the classic work by an American philosopher: Sidney Hook, *Towards the Understanding of Karl Marx: A Revolutionary Interpretation*. London: Gollancz, 1933. Half a century later, one finds another Marxist treatment by a British philosopher: Alex Callinicos, *The Revolutionary Ideas of Karl Marx*, London: Bookmarks, 1983. In addition to Callinicos, there is also the supportive treatment by Paul D'Amato, *The Meaning of Marxism*, Chicago: Haymarket Books, 2006.

For a more recent and specialized treatment by a French scholar that focuses on the thought of young Marx, see: Michael Lowy, *The Theory of Revolution in the Young Marx*, Chicago: Haymarket Books, 2005. Although in part a sensitive biography, a work that is far more an insightful and challenging interpretation is: Jerrold Seigel, *Marx's Fate: The Shape of a Life*, University Park, PA.: Penn State Press, 1993.

Less an interpretation and more of a basic reference work is the very useful: Tom Bottomore et al, *Dictionary of Marxist Thought*, Cambridge, MA, Harvard University Press, 1985. For a thoughtful collection of essays on various aspects of Marx, his theory, and legacy, see: Eric J. Hobsbawm (ed.), *The History of Marxism, Vol. I: Marxism in Marx's Day*, Bloomington: Indiana University Press, 1982. It would be easy to forget Engels' role in the life and work of Karl Marx. A correction to this tendency is: J.D. Hunley, *The Life and Thought of Friedrich Engels: A Reinterpretation*, New Haven, Ct.: Yale University Press, 1991. Hunley argues convincingly that Engels and Marx shared almost identical and appealing political views although it is curious to find such a pro-Marxist work being written by deputy command historian at the Air Training Command of the U.S. Air Force. A more recent, very nuanced and, to date, the most authoritative work in English is: Tristram Hunt, *The Frock-Coated Communist: The Revolutionary Life of Friedrich Engels*, London: Allen Lane, 2009. This work manages to bring all the contributions and contradictions of Engels to life.

C. Commentaries on Marx's Work

It is generally acknowledged that reading Marx can be rough going at first. Thus, it may be useful to consult: Peter Osborne, *How to Read Marx*, New York: W.W. Norton & Co., 2006. Of all his writings, *Das Kapital* is normally considered the hardest for beginners so one would do well to read the excellent work: Francis Wheen, *Marx's Das Kapital*, New York: Atlantic Monthly Press, 2007. Another quite serviceable resource is: Stephen Shapiro, *How to Read Marx's Capital*, London: Pluto Press, 2008. A recent quite useful work is: David Harvey, *A Companion to Marx's Capital*, London/New York: Verso, 2009.

Of all the versions of *The Communist Manifesto*, the most complete, useful, and detailed is: Phil Gasper (ed.) *The Communist Manifesto: A Road Map to History's Most Important Political Document*, Chicago: Haymarket Books, 2005.

Study Guides for Selected Works by Karl Marx

Study guides are available for the works of Marx and Engels at the Marxist Internet Archive.

The Marxist Internet Archive (MIA, http://marx.org/) is an all-volunteer, nonprofit public library, started twenty-one years ago in 1990. In 2006, MIA averaged 1.1 million visitors per month, downloading 15.5 million files per month. This represents a 25 percent increase in visitors since 2005, and a 380 percent increase in visitors since 2000.

By 2007, MIA had sixty-two active volunteers from thirty-three different countries. MIA contains the writings of 592 authors representing a complete spectrum of political, philosophical, and scientific thought, generally spanning the past two hundred years. MIA contains these writings in forty-five different languages, comprising a total size of over 53,000 documents and 29 GB of data, all created through the work of volunteers around the world.

Questions for Reflection

1. What is a proletarian?

2. How does Marx connect the fate of feudalism to the fate of landed property?

3. How could a worker become poorer, the more wealth she produces?

4. What do you make of the struggle for a shorter working week? And what about wage increases?

5. What does Marx mean by the antithesis between property and lack of property being established by private property itself?

6. What is meant by communism seeking proof for itself in the past? What's the problem with this?

7. Was Marx really an atheist? Explain why or why not.

8. In the *Communist Manifesto*, why do Marx and Engels praise capitalism?

9. What are Marx and Engels saying about "globalization" in the *Manifesto*?

10. What does Marx mean by saying, "Capital is a social relation"?

11. What is the difference between "labor" and "labor-power"?

12. In what sense did Marx argue that the dead dominate the living in capitalist society?

13. "Men make their own history, but they do not make it as they please; they do not make it under self-selected circumstances, but under circumstances existing already, given and transmitted from the past." Can you illustrate what this means in terms of current problems?

14. What does Marx mean by an object which "may have a price without having value"?

15. In what sense, are workers a social class according to Marx?

16. How would Marx explain the growing army of part-time workers today, if the capitalists need to get us working longer and longer hours?

17. How would you understand or explain the difference in wages from one country to another?

18. If Marx thought that colonization was a way out of its crisis for capitalism in his day, is this still true?

19. What in general do you think has happened to the distribution of wealth?

20. Does socialism need a phase of "primitive accumulation"?

Index